SOUTHWESTERN INDIAN TRIBES

by Tom Bahti and Mark Bahti

Tom Bahti   The late Tom Bahti, a graduate in anthropology from the University of New Mexico, started in the Indian arts business in 1949. He was nationally recognized as an authority on the arts, crafts, and culture of Southwestern Indians. He was also deeply involved in the future of the people of the Southwest.

Mark Bahti   Mark Bahti, like his father, has authored a number of books and operates an Indian arts shop in Tucson, Arizona. He is active in several Indian-run organizations that seek to provide educational and economic development opportunities for members of the Indian community.

INDEX

Introduction

Sometime before the end of the last Ice Age that covered most of North America with glaciers, there began a series of migrations out of Siberia that were to continue for thousands of years. Small bands of Stone Age hunters wandered across the land bridge that spanned the Bering Strait from Asia into the Western Hemisphere without realizing that they had discovered a new continent. These people were not all alike; they differed in physical appearance, customs, and language. The trait they did share was an ability to adapt themselves to new environments. Following ice-free valleys in pursuit of game, they drifted southward. So slowly did these movements take place that probably no single generation was conscious of the migration. Under favorable conditions bands increased in size or merged into tribes; some might settle in areas that suited them, while others would continue to wander. This process was repeated over and over again until every region, from the Arctic to the southernmost tip of South America, was inhabited.

By the time of its second discovery—this time from the east, by Europeans—the Western Hemisphere was already well-populated with diverse cultures ranging from the most rudimentary hunting and gathering economies to the highly developed civilizations of Mexico and South America.

ASIA

BERING STRAIT

GULF OF MEXICO

Early People in the Southwest

The story of people in the Southwest begins between 25,000 to 40,000 years ago with the appearance of small bands of nomads who used spears to hunt the mammoth, camel, bison, and ground sloth. Evidence of their passing is found only in stone implements they made and left in their caves and campsites, or embedded in the skeletal remains of the animals they killed.

With the retreat of the glaciers the climate slowly changed. The once-lush land, which supported the herds of animals these people hunted, became progressively drier. Lakes and swamps disappeared and streams ran intermittently. Once-plentiful game diminished, and these early hunters were forced to alter their way of life to meet these changes in their environment. They began to supplement their diet of meat with more seeds and edible plants they gathered. As plant foods became increasingly important in their diet, the rudiments of agriculture developed.

Agriculture does not allow for a nomadic existence, so these early people built semipermanent dwellings near their fields. Villages soon followed, and with them came all of the complexities of social and religious life that occur when people live together in communities.

Not all groups developed at the same pace, but contact between them increased and new ideas were exchanged. Basketry and weaving were highly developed and widespread. Pottery, a craft usually associated with sedentary, agricultural people, was either invented independently or introduced from Mexico around A.D. 100. By A.D. 600, it was known throughout the Southwest.

Movements of people still occurred, however, as local populations were subjected to droughts, erosion of farmlands, internal conflicts, or merely the human urge to move to a new area.

Cultivation of the "Sacred Triad"—corn, squash, and beans—now provided a relatively plentiful, stable food supply, and populations and villages increased in size and number. Social organization, ceremonialism, architecture, and crafts became more complex. Trade with the civilizations of Mexico grew and further enriched the lives of the peoples. By A.D. 1000, these village dwellers, or Pueblo Indians, had reached a "golden age."

Evidence of the ancestors of present-day Indians can be seen in the ruins of their pueblos and heard in the ancient oral traditions of today's tribes.

Not long after this, the ancestors of the Athabascan-speaking Navajo and Apache entered the Pueblo domain. Their constant raiding forced the Pueblo farmers to fortify their towns or abandon them entirely. Depletion of natural resources, probably internal dissension, and a prolonged drought that began in the mid-1200s, resulted in more forced migrations. By A.D. 1250, many of the great pueblos were deserted and the people had sought refuge elsewhere. When the Spaniards arrived on the scene in the mid-1500s, most of the Pueblo population was concentrated at Hopi, Zuni, Acoma, and in the Rio Grande Valley.

Between A.D. 1200 and A.D. 1400 the Piman-speaking tribes, who may be the descendants of the earlier Hohokam people, settled southern Arizona, and Yuman-speaking groups moved eastward from California into Arizona and settled along the Colorado River.

By the late 1600s most of these tribes were occupying the same areas they do today, with the Navajo and Apache people moving into the intervening areas and expanding.

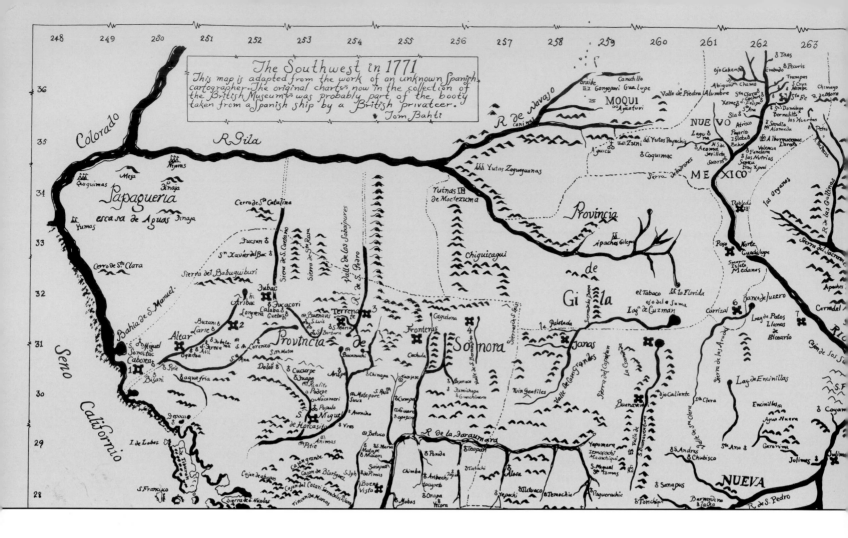

European Contact

The search for Cibola, a mythical province containing seven cities of silver and gold, brought the Spanish *conquistadores* to the Southwest. A series of explorations, beginning in 1539 with one led by Fray Marcos de Niza, failed to locate anything more spectacular than villages of mud and stone inhabited by people rich in ceremonialism but poor in material possessions.

In 1595, Juan de Oñate was awarded a contract to colonize New Mexico. Leaving from California in 1598, he arrived in New Mexico the same year to declare formal possession of Indian lands and begin colonization. The Pueblo Indians were required to swear obedience to the King of Spain and the Catholic Church. The Indians were not ousted from their lands as the Spaniards preferred to have them remain to be exploited by civil and church authorities. Tribute was demanded in the form of forced labor, food, crops, buckskins, and textiles. In return each pueblo received a Spanish name, Catholic religious instruction, and the promise of protection from Apache and Comanche raids—though much of the trouble with the marauders occurred because the Spaniards forced the Pueblo people to aid in attacks against those

tribes. Of far greater importance to the Indians was the acquisition of iron tools, fruit trees, new domestic plants, cattle, horses, and sheep.

The Spaniards also imposed the Law of the Indies which decreed that each village elect a governor, lieutenant governor, and other officials to handle secular affairs. The Indians obligingly added this new political system to their theocratic form of government, and the *cacique* or priest-chief continued to function as the real head of the village.

Life under Spanish authority became increasingly oppressive—taxation, forced labor, and harsh suppression of native religion resulted in the Great Pueblo Revolt of 1680. The tribes united in an unprecedented effort to drive out the invaders. The uprising was a success. The Spaniards retreated to El Paso and for the next 12 years the Indians once again ruled their own villages. In 1693, Diego de Vargas reconquered the Indians and reestablished Spanish authority in New Mexico.

Under Spanish rule the Indian population was centralized for ease of administration and control. In doing so, the number of pueblos in Rio Grande Valley decreased from 66 in 1540 to 19 in

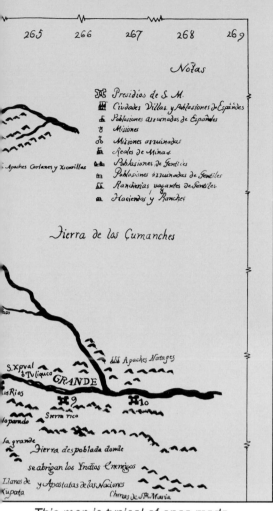

This map is typical of ones made by Europeans as a first step in claiming Indian land and dividing it up among themselves.

In 1934, the Indian Reorganization Act was passed with the idea of enabling tribes to reestablish self-government. Unfortunately, the form of self-government required by the U.S. was a non-traditional model designed for the convenience of the federal government.

Almost 20 years later, as an effort to reduce federal expenditures, a termination policy was established, which included relocations of Indians from the reservations to major urban areas across the country.

Finally, in 1975 Congress passed the Indian Self-Determination Act. Since then the tribes have sought, and often obtained, greater control over their own affairs including financial, medical, housing, educational, planning, and governance issues. The Indian Gaming Regulatory Act of 1988 has also had an immense impact on tribes in the Southwest, allowing many to boost sagging or virtually non-existent revenues and offset diminished federal funding. The new revenue source has also given tribes greater freedom to plan their futures.

1700. In this same time-frame disease, famine, and warfare reduced the native population by one-half.

The War of Independence transferred jurisdiction of New Mexico from Spain to Mexico in 1821. Mexico, unlike Spain, bestowed full rights of citizenship upon the Indians. (By contrast, the United States did not grant Indians full citizenship—the right to vote—until 1924, and Arizona and New Mexico did so only after a federal lawsuit in 1948.)

The Treaty of Guadalupe Hidalgo in 1848 marked the end of the war between the United States and Mexico, and New Mexico became a territory of the U.S. Much Indian land was lost to the new flood of settlers.

In 1849, jurisdiction over Indians was transferred from the War Department to the Bureau of Indian Affairs under the Department of the Interior, where it remains today. This transfer also marked the beginning of the reservation era, which was a policy designed to free up more land for settlement by non-Indians and to act as a "civilizing" agent.

Many Rio Grande pueblos retain as symbols of authority the silver-headed canes given them by President Lincoln in 1863. Former Taos Pueblo governor Tony Reyna holds the Lincoln cane, along with that given by King Phillip II of Spain in 1620 and ones from President Nixon (1970) and the state of New Mexico (1981).

Here at San Juan—during a Deer Dance—is evidence that while churches have a visible presence in many pueblos, the ancient traditions that preceded the European arrival remain strong.

Rio Grande Pueblos Today

Pueblo Indian life is based on the fundamental religious conviction that people must live in harmony with the natural world around them. So strong is this belief that it is not possible to separate religion from everyday life. The religious ceremonies that are held throughout the year are enactments of this philosophy.

Societies, headed by priests, within each pueblo are responsible for maintaining harmony with the supernatural world. Properly conducted ceremonies control the weather, effect cures, bring rain, mature crops, lead to success in hunting, and generally ensure that the cycle of life continues.

Harmony must also be maintained within the pueblo—family, clan, and society relationships require specific behavior of the individual, and children are reared to accept these duties. In such a tightly knit society it is not surprising to find that the welfare of the group traditionally ranks before that of the individual.

Each Tewa-speaking pueblo is divided into two groups, or moieties, known as the Winter People and the Summer People, or the Squash and

At the Tewa village of Santa Clara, the Corn Dance is observed much as it has been for centuries. At other pueblos where such ceremonies lapsed, there has been a revival of the old traditions.

MARK BAHTI

Laguna is the newest pueblo in New Mexico, founded roughly 300 years ago by survivors of the Spanish re-conquest of northern New Mexico. A Keresan-speaking pueblo, it was founded by refugees from Cochiti and Santo Domingo who were later joined by settlers from Acoma, Jemez, Oraibi, Sandia, San Felipe, Zia, and Zuni.

the Turquoise. Each moiety, under leadership of a cacique, has its own kiva and ceremonial chambers and directs the ceremonial life of the village for half of the year. Keresan-speaking pueblos have only one cacique who is responsible for the spiritual well-being of the entire pueblo. Ordinarily, it is he who selects the officers to handle secular affairs. Each pueblo is politically autonomous.

Although the Catholic Church has claimed converts among the Rio Grande pueblos for over 300 years, and most of the Indians make use of some services provided by the church (baptism, confirmation, marriage, burial), the importance of native religion has not diminished. The two religions coexist and the Indians find nothing inconsistent in making use of both.

In recent years there has been a revival in the native religions—old ceremonies have been renewed and more people, especially younger members, participate in the ceremonial life of the pueblos.

Problems that face the pueblos are serious and numerous. Increased intermarriage with non-Indians tends to weaken pueblo authority. Population increases render present land resources inadequate. Outmoded and inequitable systems of land inheritance have fractionalized holdings until they have become impractical to farm. Agriculture, once the economic foundation of pueblo life, has become less and less important, being supplanted by other forms of economic development ranging from resorts, golf courses, and casinos, to shopping centers and even housing developments aimed at non-Indian markets.

Encroachments from non-Indian cultures combined with internal frictions, factionalism, and substance abuse, all symptoms of a culture under pressure and in the process of social change, weaken tribal solidarity.

A strong love for the tribal lands, a common language, and a deep attachment to and respect for the religious life of the village seem to hold each pueblo group together in the face of these difficulties.

Life in the pueblos is neither ideal nor idyllic, but it obviously holds a greater attraction and greater satisfaction for most of these people than an existence in the mainstream of American life.

These Indian tribes have not only survived 400 years of occupation by alien cultures, but have managed to retain more of their native life than they have lost. It is probably not overly optimistic to believe that they can continue in the same manner.

ACOMA

(ah'-ko-mah) — from the native word *Ah'-ku-me*, meaning "people of the white rock." Language: Keresan. Reservation: 378,345 acres. Population: 5,029. Government: Cacique chooses secular officers and council members. Dances: Sept. 2 - Harvest Dance and annual Feast Day of San Estevan. Dec. 24 - Christmas Eve festival.

Acoma, the Southwest's "Sky City," is located atop a mesa that stands nearly 400 feet above the surrounding valley. Acoma vies with the Hopi pueblo of Oraibi for the claim to being "the oldest continuously inhabited community in the U.S." Archaeological evidence indicates that the site has been occupied since at least A.D. 1150.

The first Europeans to visit the pueblo were part of Coronado's expedition, who arrived in 1540. At the time there were 5,000 Acoma occupying several villages in the area.

The Spaniards feared Acoma's military potential and its control over neighboring pueblos. In 1599, the Spanish territorial governor Juan de Oñate sent a military force to demand tribute and supplies. The Acoma responded by attacking the soldiers. The following month a larger force was sent to lay siege to Acoma. Over a three-day battle, 800 Indians were slaughtered and the mesa-top town largely destroyed. The survivors were taken captive and marched to Santo Domingo Pueblo to stand trial. Women over 12 years of age were sentenced to 20 years slave labor; men between 12 and 25 received the same fate in addition to having one foot chopped off. (Those over 25 were deemed too old for 20 years of servitude, and so had one foot amputated before being sent home.) Young girls were given to the Church, and the boys to the officer who led the soldiers as a reward for his victory.

In 1629, the Franciscans established the mission of San Estevan del Rey at the pueblo under the direction of Fray Ramirez. This impressive structure, which has been rebuilt and remodeled many times, loses some of its charm when it is remembered that it was originally built (like most church buildings at Indian pueblos) with forced labor. The enormous logs that form the beamed ceiling, for example, were carried from Mount Taylor, which lies a hard two days walk from the village.

Acoma participated in the Great Pueblo Revolt of 1680, and later served as a refuge from the Spaniards for other Indians. During the reconquest, the Spanish attacked Acoma in 1696 and laid waste their fields to try and starve them into submission. It was three years before Acoma was finally forced to submit to Spanish authority.

Only a few families live in the mesa-top village year-round. Most occupy the permanent farming communities of Acomita, Anzac, and McCartys. All of them, however, return to the main pueblo for ceremonies.

Farming, ranching, wage work, and some mining are the primary occupations. Uranium mining, once the major source of tribal income, has collapsed. A casino is now providing a source of considerable income as well as employment for the Acoma people. Lakes built for recreation were polluted by communities and mining activities upstream, forcing the Acoma to shut down the lakes, drain, and dredge them. They are now in the process of refilling the lakes, which they hope will become a significant source of income.

Acoma has long been noted for producing very fine polychrome pottery with the thinnest walls of any Pueblo pottery, but corrugated pots are also made. This corrugated vessel by Corinne Garcia is meant to represent the rock cisterns atop the mesa which catch run-off rainwater. While no longer vital to the existence of the pueblo, they are still an attraction for children—and visitors.

The best-known craft of Acoma Pueblo is pottery. Many potters still produce large quantities of carefully painted, thin-walled ware. In addition to the traditional jars and bowl forms, copies of prehistoric vessels, figurines of animals, birds, and humans are produced. Several potters are producing new, innovative forms. Most potters use conventional kilns to fire their work, and a number have begun to paint and fire ready-made "greenware."

Visitors to Acoma are charged an admission fee (a practice begun in 1928), which includes a guide and transportation up and down the mesa in a bus. Picture-taking anywhere on Acoma land also requires payment of a fee.

The high mesa upon which Acoma rests provided security and protection from its enemies for over 400 years. In 1599 Spanish soldiers lay siege to the pueblo killing hundreds and brutally mistreating the survivors.

Famous for their pottery, Acoma artists still produce vessels shaped like the ones once used to hold water, store seeds, and serve food. Acoma used to be known for its beautifully woven and embroidered mantas or dresses, but textile arts have disappeared here as at most other pueblos.

K. C. DEN DOOVEN

ISLETA (iss-leh´-tah) — from the Spanish word for "little island." Native name is *Cheh-wib-ahg,* meaning "flint kick-stick place." Both names are descriptive of the physical location of the pueblo. Language: Tiwa. Reservation: 211,103 acres. Population: 4,105. Government: Constitution adopted in 1947. Adult members (women received the vote in 1971) annually elect governor, president, and vice-president of the council. These officers then select council members and minor officials. Dances: Jan. 3 - Corn and Turtle Dance. Aug. 28 - Corn Dance and fiesta. Sept. 4 - San Agustin Feast Day. Dec. 24 - Christmas Eve dance. ▬▬▬

Unlike other Rio Grande pueblos, Isleta legend states that their ancestors came from the south as well as the north. The present site has been occupied since the early 1700s, and may have been used at least seasonally since the early 1500s.

The population of Isleta was greatly increased in the 1600s by an influx of refugees from other Tiwa villages who sought protection from Apache raids. In 1680, the population was estimated to be 2,000. Of the 20 villages that comprised the Southern Tiwa province at the time of Spanish contact, only Isleta remained by the late 1700s.

The large numbers of Spanish settlers who moved to Isleta prior to the 1680 revolt unwittingly prevented that village from taking part in the initial uprising. However, before the fleeing Spanish reached Isleta on their retreat south to El Paso, most of the villagers had abandoned their pueblo and joined the insurgents.

In 1681, Governor Otermin, during an unsuccessful reconquest attempt, attacked several Southern Tiwa villages including Isleta. He took hundreds of captives south to El Paso, where he settled them at a new village called Ysleta del Sur. Other Isletans fled to the safety of the Hopi pueblos, not returning until some 35 years later.

In 1880, a group of religious conservatives fleeing strife at their pueblo of Laguna were invited to settle at Isleta. Though many left a few years later, the religious leader stayed, along with the katsina masks and other religious objects.

Isleta was the only Rio Grande pueblo to adopt the Spanish custom of electing a governor. This caused a certain amount of confusion in leadership since it usurped the power of the cacique who ordinarily selected secular officials. By the late 1800s factionalism developed over the issues of leadership in village affairs and election procedures. It reached a peak in the early 1940s. A constitution and council form of government, adopted in 1947, did not solve the question.

Problems continued and in 1971 women were enfranchised as part of an effort to resolve these issues. Despite its factionalism, Isleta maintains a full and active ceremonial life, and is now moving forward on economic development for the community and dealing with the pressures brought on by the steady southward expansion of the city of Albuquerque. The urban encroachment and industrial development has created pollution problems downstream at Isleta, affecting water for drinking, farming, and several small fishing and recreational lakes owned by the pueblo.

Agriculture is a community enterprise, though many still maintain their own garden plots and raise stock. Profits from tribal gaming, a small industrial park, cattle grazing, and wage work are the primary sources of income. Some jewelry and pottery is produced. What is known as Isleta pottery is made by descendants of the Laguna colony who settled at Isleta in 1880.

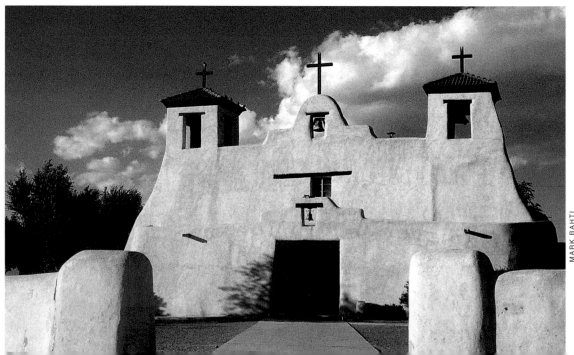

Portions of the original structure, built after the Great Pueblo Revolt of 1680, are incorporated in the church of San Antonio de la Isleta. Of the 20 Tiwa Indian villages that existed in New Mexico before the revolt, only one, Isleta, remained by the late 1700s.

MARK BAHTI

YSLETA DEL SUR (iss-leh′-tah del sur) —

from the Spanish for "South Isleta." Language: Tiwa. Reservation: 119 acres. Population: 1,473. Government: Elected and appointed officials include cacique, cacique teniente, alguacil, and war captain. The cacique and war captain are appointed for life. The other positions are filled by election each New Year's Eve. Dances: June 13 - St. Anthony's Feast Day. ━━━━━━━

Both the text and the carved Indian image are in error. The Tiwa who settled in El Paso are generally believed to have been forced to accompany the Spanish.

Founded in 1681 by Tiwas from Isleta Pueblo, most of whom were forced to accompany the Spanish who fled the Great Pueblo Revolt, most tribal members still recognize Isleta as the ancestral pueblo. Inhabitants also include Piro and Manso Indians. The mission of Corpus Christi de la Ysleta del Sur (dedicated to Our Lady of Mount Carmel) was built in 1681, and remains the focal point of the Tigua (Tiwa) Indian community.

The Tiwas helped defend El Paso against Comanche and Apache raids, and for this service were awarded a land grant from the King of Spain in 1751. After the Americans assumed control of Texas, the Indians of Isleta found their land steadily being lost to encroaching settlers and speculators who used everything from the state legislature to outright theft. The tribe was recognized by the state of Texas in 1967 and by the federal government in 1968, but was placed under state jurisdiction for many years.

Tradition holds that katsina-like beings live in the nearby Cerro Alto mountains. Called *Awelos* (from the Spanish word for grandparents—*abuelos*), they protect the tribe and punish wrongdoers. They are represented by two dancers who wear buffalo hide masks. The masks, along with the tribal drum, are kept in the *tusla*, a building used primarily for religious purposes. The tribal drum has special significance for it is said to have been brought from Isleta in 1680.

In 1971, virtually every family's income was below the poverty level. In recent years, development of shops, a museum, a recreation area at Hueco Tanks, a restaurant, and a casino operation have greatly improved living conditions among the Tiguas. There has been a modest revival of some craftwork and the introduction of wheel-thrown pottery.

Also associated with the Tigua of El Paso is the Tiwa community of Tortugas in Las Cruces, New Mexico, which does not have state or federal recognition. Run by a community corporation (composed of Indians and non-Indians) founded in 1914, they own 40 acres on which half of the tribal members live. Many tribal members are enrolled members of the tribe at Ysleta del Sur.

Since only a fraction of the lands taken from the Tigua of Ysleta del Sur have been returned, their casino has been the centerpiece of economic revival efforts.

LEE MARMON

The Catholic Mission at Laguna was built a few years after the pueblo was founded. The interior incorporates both Catholic and Indian motifs. A Presbyterian mission, built over a century and a half later, brought deep dissension. Bitter factionalism developed and, when an outsider was elected as the governor of the village, traditional Laguna religious leaders closed their kivas in protest and moved to the pueblo of Isleta.

LAGUNA (lah-goo'-nah) — Spanish word for "lake." Native name is *Kawaik*, from the word for "lake." Language: Keresan. Reservation: 528,684 acres. Population: 7,316. Government: Secular officers, with a tribal council headed by a governor. Constitution adopted in 1958. Dances: June 24 - San Juan's Day. Aug. 10 - Corn Dance. Sept. 19 - Harvest Dance. Dec. 24 - Christmas Eve Dance.

Laguna, founded in 1699, is the most recent of New Mexico's pueblos. It was built by rebels from Cochiti and Santo Domingo who survived de Vargas's attack on their stronghold at La Cieneguilla in 1694. Later they were joined by members of other pueblos—the clans at Laguna trace their origins to Acoma, Zuni, San Felipe, Zia, Oraibi, Sandia, and Jemez.

The population of Laguna, formerly concentrated at the mother village, now also occupies seven nearby settlements: Paguate, Encinal, Paraje, New Laguna, Mesita, Casa Blanca, and Seama. The latter community includes three "suburbs" named Harrisburg, Philadelphia, and New York.

Governor Cubero, who visited the pueblo in the year of its founding, named it San Jose de la Laguna. A mission was built at the village in 1706.

The introduction of Presbyterianism to Laguna in 1870, by two Anglos who had married Laguna women, resulted in bitter factionalism. A Presbyterian mission was built at the pueblo in 1875, and the new sect succeeded in electing an outsider to the position of village governor. In protest the conservatives closed their kivas, removed their religious objects, and left the pueblo. Most of them moved to Isleta where they founded the colony of Oraibi. A few took up residence at Mesita. The exodus left Laguna without traditional religious-based leadership.

The tribal government of Laguna was one of the first and most "progressive" of all the pueblos. For many years, beginning in the late 1950s, there was sizeable income from uranium leases which was invested in scholarship programs and local projects as well as individual disbursements. (Pollution from radioactive tailings is the other legacy from uranium mining, which ended in 1983.) Laguna Industries, located in a building previously occupied by an electronics plant initially underwritten by the tribe, continues to offer employment in the community. Among those who have contracts with the plant is the Department of Defense. Additionally, the tribe operates a construction company. For most tribal members, wage work combined with some farming and ranching are the primary sources of income. Sheepherding was once the major source of wealth for the pueblo, but overgrazing took its toll on the land and, in 1935, the federal government ordered the flocks reduced by over 70 percent.

Today, little craftwork is produced except for some embroidery and a limited amount of pottery and jewelry.

SANDIA (sahn-dee'-yah) — Spanish word for "watermelon" and for the nearby mountains. Native name is *Nafiat*, meaning "sandy place." Language: Tiwa. Reservation: 22,871 acres. Population: 368. Government: Cacique appoints secular officers. Dances: June 13 - Corn Dance and feast day. Dec. 31 - New Year's Eve Deer Dance.

The pueblo of Sandia dates from about A.D. 1300. Remains of the early village visited by Coronado in 1540 are still visible near the present church.

In the early 17th century, the Franciscans built the mission of San Francisco at the village. It was destroyed during the Great Pueblo Revolt in 1680. (The existing church was built in the early 1890s.)

Fearing Spanish reprisals the Sandia people abandoned their pueblo after the rebellion and took refuge with the Hopis. (Their fears were well founded as in 1681, during an unsuccessful reconquest attempt, the Spanish sacked and burned the pueblo.) On Second Mesa, north of the pueblo of Mishongnovi, they established the village of Payupki, where they lived until 1742 when two Spanish priests persuaded 500 of them to return to New Mexico. They reestablished their village on the site of the old one. The new pueblo was named Nuestra Señora de los Dolores y San Antonio de Sandia—the Hopis call it Payupki.

Despite its proximity to Albuquerque, Sandia has kept a low profile through this century, and little is known about its traditional beliefs and practices.

Farming has declined in importance, being supplanted by wage work. Tribal income and employment is derived from a successful arts and crafts enterprise, fishing fees, and a casino.

Sandia is a conservative pueblo where traditional Pueblo dress such as this manta is still generally worn during religious observances. They are very protective of their privacy. Though their land is virtually surrounded by development and they have built a casino and craft shop along the interstate, Sandia Pueblo does not encourage visitors and closes all access during ceremonies. There are no signs marking the way to Sandia Pueblo.

SANTA ANA (sahn'tah ahn'ah) — Spanish name for Saint Anne. Native name is *Tamaya*. Language: Keresan. Reservation: 61,931 acres. Population: 595. Government: Cacique selects secular officers annually. Council includes all adult male family heads. Dances: June 24 - San Juan's Day. July 26 - Green Corn Dance and Feast Day.

Oñate visited Tamaya, which he renamed Santa Ana, in 1598, and a mission was built there in the 17th century. In 1680, Santa Ana, San Felipe, and Santo Domingo joined forces during the Great Pueblo Revolt.

The governor of El Paso led an attack on Santa Ana in 1687 during a reconquest attempt, and burned the village. Those who escaped joined with survivors from Zia to establish a village on Red Mesa near Jemez as a defense against the Spanish. In 1692, de Vargas persuaded them to return to Santa Ana and rebuild the village. After this they remained loyal to Spanish rule and, as a result, suffered periodic raids by the Jemez people who wanted all pueblos to continue to resist Spanish rule. The present church at Santa Ana dates from 1734, but may include portions of the earlier mission.

A lack of agricultural land and water for irrigation has forced virtual abandonment of the pueblo of Santa Ana. Most of the tribe now lives at Ranchitos (also known as Ranchos de Santa Ana), a farming community on the Rio Grande near Bernalillo. The pueblo began buying farming land in this area in the early 1700s. Only a few people remain behind year-round to take care of the pueblo.

One of the seven Keresan-speaking pueblos, Santa Ana remains active ceremonially, and the people return to their village to perform their ceremonies. At all other times the pueblo remains closed to non-tribal members. After a series of devastating epidemics in the early 1900s, the population has recovered and is growing. Agriculture remains important, though the tribe has also developed a restaurant, golf course, and casino which provide revenue as well as employment.

Traditional pottery, revived twice since the 1940s, is not currently being made.

Most of the people of Santa Ana live east of the pueblo, in Ranchitos, along the Rio Grande. They return to the pueblo for traditional ceremonies, but only a few live there year-round. For this reason, it is closed to outsiders for all but a few days annually; hence, the very permanent-looking sign.

Without forgetting their past, many pueblos near urban areas are creating a new economic future. The country club and golf resort developed by Santa Ana overlooks an ancient pueblo past while providing an income for the tribe's present and future.

SAN FELIPE (sahn feh-lee'-pay) — Spanish name for Saint Philip. Native name is *Katishtya*. Language: Keresan. Reservation: 48,930 acres. Population: 2,516. Government: Religious leader selects secular officers and council. Dances: Feb. 2 - Buffalo Dance. May 1 - Feast Day and Corn Dance. June 29 - San Pedro's Day celebration. Dec. 24 - Christmas Eve Dance.

Tradition holds that the people of San Felipe and Cochiti once were one, living in a pueblo known as Kuapa. The aggressive expansion of the Tewa people to the north eventually forced abandonment of the pueblo, with the group splitting and going on to found separate villages.

The present pueblo of San Felipe, which was established by 1706, is the fourth village to bear the native name Katishtya. The first, located farther south, was abandoned before the Spaniards arrived. The second, named San Felipe by the Spanish in 1591, was on the east bank of the Rio Grande at the foot of La Mesita, across the river from a second village belonging to these Keresan people. Here, in the early 1600s, a mission was established and maintained until the Great Pueblo Revolt of 1680 when the villagers destroyed the church and abandoned their pueblo.

Fearful of Spanish reprisals, the people of San Felipe joined forces with refugees from several other pueblos at La Cieneguilla, a fortified site north of Cochiti.

In 1693, General de Vargas persuaded the residents to leave their fortress. The third village of Katishtya was then established in a defensive position on the top of Black Mesa on the west side of the Rio Grande. San Felipe remained obedient to the Spanish thereafter and provided warriors to aid the Spaniards in subduing the other pueblo tribes. This village was abandoned in 1700, and the present town built below the mesa along the Rio Grande.

San Felipe shares with Santo Domingo a reputation for being a very conservative village. The cacique, aided by a war captain and his assistant, annually appoints all secular officers and council members. This form of government precludes elections and limits participation in village affairs by its younger members. The number of young people who leave the pueblo to seek outside employment has risen steadily for years.

Farming, which has declined in importance as an economic pursuit, may improve if present plans for land and water distribution are carried out.

What is thought of as traditional San Felipe pottery has disappeared. New traditions, based in part on the old, and using traditional clays and paints, have emerged. As in most pueblos, pottery art is replacing pottery utensils. Hubert Candelario

San Felipe has always been noted among the Rio Grande pueblos for its beautiful ceremonial dances and, in recent years, a number of old rituals have been revived.

Traditional pottery has disappeared, but a limited amount of very innovative pottery is made. Other than that, no significant amount of craftwork is produced.

The plaza in front of the present church (built in 1890) at Santo Domingo Pueblo is the site of many traditional religious observances during the year. For this reason, photographs of the church are no longer permitted.

SANTO DOMINGO (sahn'-toh doh-ming'-oh) — Spanish for Saint Dominic. Native name is *Giuwa*. Language: Keresan. Reservation: 71,093 acres. Population: 4,949. Government: Council made up of former governors chooses secular officers annually. Strong control exerted over village government by religious leaders. Dances: June 29 - San Pedro's Day celebration. Aug. 4 - Corn Dance and Feast Day. Dec. 24 - Christmas Eve Dance. ▬▬▬▬▬

Santo Domingo has long been regarded as one of the most conservative of all the pueblos. The people are friendly but independent, maintaining a high degree of tribal unity in government and religious affairs despite outside pressures to change.

The present pueblo of Santo Domingo dates to about 1700. A disastrous flood in 1886 destroyed much of the town and its church. It was soon rebuilt and a new church (the present one) constructed in 1890. Floods have always been a particular menace to the villagers—at least three of their earlier towns and two Spanish missions have been destroyed by Rio Grande floodwaters.

Oñate visited Santo Domingo in 1598 and met there with the leaders of more than 30 pueblos. Whether they fully understood that the Spaniards were claiming their land is not known

(and not likely), but Oñate claimed that he had received pledges of allegiance to both the Crown and the Church from all those assembled.

Alonza Catiti, an interpreter from Santo Domingo, was one of the three leaders of the Great Pueblo Revolt of 1680. The village was abandoned at that time and the people moved to a fortified position, La Cieneguilla, in anticipation of a Spanish counterattack. In 1683, most of them returned to their village.

The Santo Domingans resisted reconquest by the Spaniards—they destroyed their pueblo in 1692 and joined forces with the Indians of Jemez. Their new village near Jemez was destroyed by de Vargas two years later, and many of the people were taken captive. Some who escaped fled to the Hopi villages, and others who had remained with the rebels at La Cieneguilla moved to Acoma country with some Cochiti refugees where they established the new pueblo of Laguna.

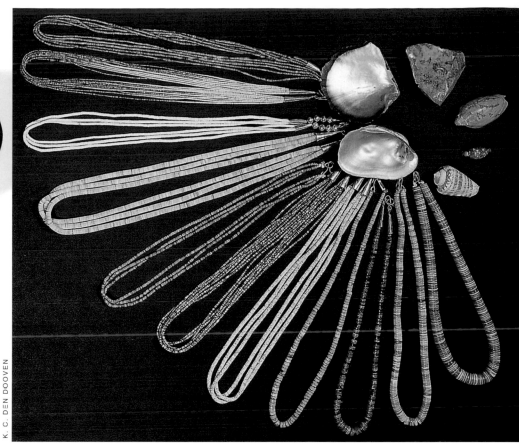

While there are Santo Domingo ceramists creating art pottery, traditional forms remain strong. Water jars, storage vessels, and stew bowls—both individual and communal—are regularly made, and the stew bowls are often used during feast days.

K. C. DEN DOOVEN

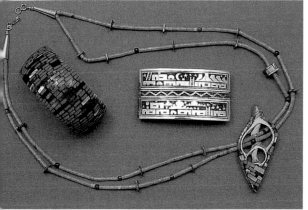

At one time stone and shell bead necklaces were made in all the pueblos, but by the latter half of the 1900s most were being made at Santo Domingo Pueblo. A number of silversmiths are also active at Santo Domingo.

Santo Domingo was later resettled by de Vargas's captives and those who returned from Hopi country. A number of Tano Indians from the Galisteo Basin—refugees from the Comanche raids—also joined the pueblo.

As far as was possible the people followed a policy of passive resistance toward the Spanish. Native ceremonies were carried on in secrecy in defiance of the Catholic church. Their present dislike for those who would pry into native rituals is probably a direct carry-over from those times.

Modern conveniences and technology, from running water to computers, are much in evidence at the pueblo, but the people resist any change that would alter their fundamental way of life and religion.

The economy of the pueblo is based on subsistence farming, cattle raising, wage work, and fire fighting. An outlet mall and other economic development programs are broadening and strengthening the tribe's economic base.

Many villagers supplement their incomes with craftwork. Pottery and silver jewelry are produced, but the best-known crafts are beads of shell and turquoise. These necklaces (erroneously called "wampum" by some) are known as *heishe*, from the word in their language for shell. Their work is much in demand by Indians of other tribes—as a result many Santo Domingan craftspeople have become something of itinerant salespeople. (As early as 1850 they were reported trading with tribes in Oklahoma.) It is not uncommon to find these Indians selling their work throughout the United States.

It is difficult not to admire the Santo Domingans—and other Indians—who resist the pressures which would change their distinctive life to that uniformly gray existence of the "average citizen."

This Corn Maiden, by Marie Romero of Jemez, is an expression of the fundamental importance of corn in Pueblo Indian life.

JEMEZ (hay'-mez) — Spanish spelling of the native word *Hemish*, meaning "the people." Native name for the pueblo is *Walatowa*, which means "village of the canyon." Language: Towa. Reservation: 89,624 acres. Population: 2,588. Government: Cacique selects secular officers, including governor and lieutenant governor. Tribal council composed of former governors. Dances: June 24 - San Juan's Day. Aug. 2 - Old Pecos Feast Day and Dance. Nov. 12 - Harvest Dance and Feast Day.

This Towa-speaking tribe inhabited a number of villages on the tributaries of the Jemez River before moving into the main Jemez Valley. At the time of Spanish contact in 1541, they were living in 11 small villages in the Agua Caliente region.

In accordance with the Spanish policy of consolidating Indian populations wherever possible, the Jemez people were persuaded to abandon most of their pueblos so that by 1625 they were concentrated in only two villages. In each of these the Spaniards established a mission.

From their earliest contacts the tribe maintained a hostile attitude toward the Spanish invaders. Two unsuccessful uprisings against Spanish authority occurred at Jemez before the Great Pueblo Revolt of 1680.

Spanish efforts to reconquer Jemez were thwarted as villagers retreated to fortified positions on the nearby mesa whenever soldiers appeared. From this stronghold they sent out raiding parties to harass Santa Ana and the Zia for siding with the Spaniards.

In 1694, de Vargas, with the help of Indian allies from Santa Ana, Zia, and San Felipe, attacked and destroyed their mesa village. The survivors of this battle resettled one of their villages in the valley. Women and children who were taken captive were allowed to return only after the Jemez warriors helped the Spanish defeat the Tewas living at Black Mesa.

Before long, however, the Jemez had enlisted military aid from the Zuni, Acoma, and Navajo tribes and resumed their hostilities against pueblos to the south who had sided with the Spanish. The Jemez Rebellion was finally crushed, and those who escaped found refuge among the Navajo and the Hopi. (The *Hemis* katsina, a popular figure at the Niman ceremony of the Hopi, was introduced to them by the Jemez people at that time.)

In 1703, most of the people returned to the Jemez Valley and built their present village at the site of an earlier settlement.

In 1838, they were joined by the remaining 17 inhabitants of Pecos, another Towa-speaking pueblo located further to the east, near the edge of the plains. (Disease, warfare, and constant raiding had decimated their numbers, forcing abandonment.) Even today their individuality is still acknowledged—through the creation of the position of second lieutenant governor, filled by the governor of the Pecos immigrants.

Although many families farm small garden plots, agriculture is becoming less important to the pueblo's economy. Cattle raising, seasonal wage work, and a renaissance in pottery work provide income, but unemployment remains high at Jemez because of its distance from urban areas.

Plaited bowl-shaped baskets of yucca, pottery, storyteller figurines, and sculpture as well as some embroidery and jewelry are the arts and crafts presently produced at the pueblo.

The tribal fair at Jemez Pueblo is a continuation of the intertribal trade that has characterized Pueblo life for centuries. While trade goes on throughout the year, it is at its most intense during ceremonial events.

ZIA (tsee'-ah) — from the native name *Tseya*. Language: Keresan. Reservation: 121,600 acres. Population: 736 (resident 613). Government: Cacique selects governor who appoints committee to handle secular affairs. Council is made up of all adult males. Dances: Aug. 15 - Corn Dance and Feast Day of Our Lady of Asuncion.

Early Spanish accounts refer to Zia as the most populous (2,500+) and most important town in a province containing five pueblos. Oñate visited the pueblo in 1598, and shortly thereafter the mission of Nuestra Senora de la Asuncion de Sia was established.

Zia took an active part in the Great Pueblo Revolt and defied Spanish attempts at reconquest. In 1689, Governor Domingo de Cruzate attacked Zia, and in a bloody battle killed more than 600 Indians, destroyed the town, and sold the captives into slavery. Those who escaped built a new pueblo near Jemez where they stayed until 1692 when de Vargas induced them to return to Zia and rebuild the pueblo and its church. From this time on they remained friendly to the Spaniards and often served as allies in attacks on other pueblos. This loyalty to the Spanish did not endear them to other tribes, and Zia frequently found itself the target of punitive raids by neighboring pueblos. Even today that alliance with the Spanish is unfavorably remembered by some from the other pueblos.

Because of inadequate land and water, Zia has been a poor pueblo in historic times. Limited cattle raising and farming goes on, but wage work in nearby communities accounts for most of the pueblo's income.

Internal strife has plagued Zia. In the 1930s, a group of Zias living in Albuquerque joined an evangelical sect of faith healers. The converts returned to the pueblo seeking new members, but after much controversy they returned to Albuquerque. Other factionalism resulted in the burning of a kiva belonging to a rival group.

Faced by a shortage of land, an increasing population, and continuing unrest, the future of Zia is unclear.

Zia potters are widely known for their fine polychrome ware, which is traded to Indians and non-Indians alike. New Mexico's state flag is derived from a Zia pottery design. Zia artists almost lost the right to the Zia sun symbol design when a large corporation nearly succeeded in obtaining the copyright to it.

Traditional Zia pottery often incorporates bird designs. The Zia sun symbol is their most famous pottery motif and it graces the New Mexico state flag.

Classic Zia pottery—like these examples by the Medina family—is black and red on a cream- or sand-colored slip with a red base, with bird, plant, and cloud motifs.

MARK BAHTI

Storytelling is one of the most ancient of traditions, but making storyteller figurines only dates back to 1964 when Helen Cordero made one in memory of her grandfather. Cochiti Pueblo is famous for its figurines generally and its storyteller figurines specifically, which have almost completely replaced traditional Cochiti pottery. These were made by Buffy Cordero, a granddaughter of the woman who began this figurative style.

COCHITI (ko'-chi-tee) — Spanish version of the native name *Kotyete*. Language: Keresan. Reservation: 50,681 acres. Population: 1,057. Government: Religious hierarchy selects secular officers annually. The Tribal Council is made up of former officers. Dances: June 13 - San Antonio's Day Dance. June 24 - San Juan's Day celebration. July 14 - Corn Dance and San Buenaventura Feast Day.

Before the arrival of the Spanish, the people of Cochiti and San Felipe had formed a single tribe. Warfare with their Tewa neighbors caused a split, and the two groups established separate villages in A.D. 1250. The present pueblo of Cochiti dates from this period.

Oñate visited Cochiti in 1598. The mission of San Buenaventura was built there in 1628. Although extensively remodeled many times since it was rebuilt in the 18th century, the present church still contains sections of the original.

The Cochiti people abandoned their pueblo after the 1680 Revolt, and retreated to the fortified village of La Cieneguilla with Indians from Santo Domingo, Taos, San Felipe, and Picuris.

In 1692, this band of insurgents promised de Vargas that they would return to their villages peacefully. Only San Felipe kept its promise—the others decided to continue their resistance. Under cover of darkness, de Vargas's soldiers and their Indian allies attacked the rebels, destroyed the village, and took many prisoners. Cochiti was not resettled until 1694.

During the late 1700s and early 1800s, Cochiti served as a refuge for Spanish and Mexican colonists from Navajo and Apache raids. As a result there has been considerable intermarriage between the two groups. Even today a few families of Spanish-American descent still live in the pueblo.

Conservative and progressive groups are present in Cochiti with control of village affairs in the hands of the conservatives for many years. Serious factionalism was avoided by urging progressive members to participate in the council discussions even though many did not take part in ceremonial affairs. In recent years the division between the two groups has faded, and there has been increased participation in the traditional religious life of the pueblo. Cochiti maintains a full ceremonial calendar which includes a number of katsina dances not open to the public.

Agriculture was an important economic activity at Cochiti, but is now limited to garden plots and alfalfa fields. The completion of Cochiti Dam provided a new development base that includes fishing, boating, housing, and golfing. These activities are the major sources of revenue for the tribe.

Drums and pottery—primarily the storyteller figurines, which originated here—are the best-known Cochiti crafts. Though not widespread, there is a long tradition of fine silverwork from this pueblo. Cochiti drums, noted for their superior workmanship and fine tone, are very popular with other tribes.

Cochiti is famous among all the pueblos for its excellent drums, used during religious dances held in the plazas as well as ceremonies in the kivas—and sold to the non-Indian trade. It is not unusual for a fine drum to be used for decades. Ysleta del Sur has one that dates back to the late 1600s. Making a fine, durable drum with a good "voice" is an art—generally passed down through the generations—and involves an extended apprenticeship. Arnold Herrera learned from his father, Jim, a very well-respected drum maker—and is in turn teaching his sons.

Traditional foods are an important part of any culture, and the pueblos are no exception. Anyone who has visited Cochiti or any other pueblo when a ceremony was being held knows why they are often referred to as Feast Days. Pueblo bread, baked in an earthen oven called an horno, is a staple of such meals.

TESUQUE (teh-soo'-kay)

— Spanish pronunciation of the native name *Te-tsu-geh*, meaning "cottonwood tree place." Language: Tewa. Reservation: 16,811 acres. Population: 400. Government: Religious leaders choose secular officers annually. Dances: Nov. 12 - San Diego Feast Day and Dance. Dec. 24 - Christmas Eve Dance.

Tesuque has probably occupied two separate sites in historic times. Their first village was located three miles west of the present pueblo. It was abandoned, and its 17th-century mission destroyed during the Great Pueblo Revolt of 1680. Tesuque struck the first blow of the rebellion and took part in the general attack on Santa Fe—after this the villagers scattered to join other rebel Tewas at Black Mesa and La Cieneguilla, and did not return to reestablish their village until the early 1700s.

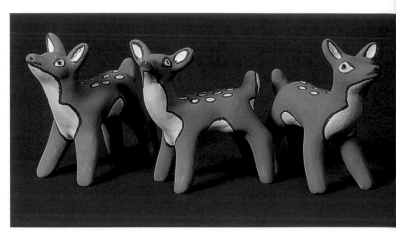

Blue deer by Tesuque potter Bea Tioux reflect the blue deer often seen in Indian paintings of an earlier era— from the 1930s until the early 1970s.

The pueblo of Tesuque has kept much of its old way of life—religious and political leadership remain in the hands of the two caciques, the heads of the village's Winter and Summer moieties. Nevertheless, they maintain a practical and progressive attitude by appointing capable young men to those secular offices that handle business affairs outside the pueblo.

Tesuque produced a very creditable pottery, but the craft disappeared in the early 1900s and the potters began to cater to the American tourist by turning out clay knickknacks decorated with poster paints. The most infamous of these was the so-called Tesuque Rain God, which was originally produced as a giveaway for a Midwestern candy manufacturer. Probably patterned after a figurine from Old Mexico, it had no connection with rain, Tesuque, or their religion. Traditional pottery, made from a micaceous clay, has been revived in recent years. Stock raising, wage work, some farming, gaming, and tourism are currently the primary sources of tribal income.

Figurines known as "rain gods" are still made at Tesuque. They are not rain gods, however. The first ones were made roughly a century ago—commissioned by a Santa Fe curio dealer for a Midwestern candy manufacturer who used them in a promotional scheme. The candy is no longer made, but the figures still are. Duran family

POJOAQUE (po-hwah'-key) — Spanish pronunciation of the native name *Posunwage*, meaning "drinking water place." Language: Tewa. Reservation: 11,601 acres. Population: 285. Government: Governor and lieutenant governor elected annually along with two other officials. Council is made up of past tribal officials. Dances: Dec. 12 - Feast of Guadalupe, fiesta and dance.

Currently the smallest of the six Tewa pueblos, Pojoaque was a very large pueblo in the 1300s. Its population suffered greatly after the Great Pueblo Revolt and during the reconquest. The tribe was decimated and the pueblo abandoned. Five families reestablished it in 1706, but the population never rose past 100. It was almost destroyed by a smallpox epidemic in 1890 and, combined with steady encroachment on their best farmland by non-Indians, the pueblo was again abandoned by about 1912. Traditional Pojoaque culture virtually disappeared. In 1933, some of the land was restored. At that time fewer than 40 descendants could be found, and only 14 were willing to move back.

The reservation was established in 1934 for the descendants of the original pueblo. This group forms the unit which handles the leasing of its commercial holdings on the highway between Santa Fe and Española, and development of the gaming enterprises as well as a travel agency, a construction company, and a visitor complex that includes a gift shop, museum, and restaurant.

At one time there was nothing in the appearance of this village to distinguish it from any other rural community in northern New Mexico. As part of an effort to revitalize traditional Pojoaque culture, a new kiva has been built. Several painters and silversmiths are active, and pottery making is enjoying a resurgence.

Some of Pojoaque's inhabitants participate in the dances of neighboring Tewa-speaking pueblos. No photography, sketching, or recording of any sort is allowed.

Pojoaque pottery, made from a mica-flecked clay, has been widely traded for centuries. This durable, thin-walled pottery is sought after by both Indians and non-Indians. It is prized for its utilitarian qualities as well as for its aesthetic merits. Cordelia and Glen Gomez

Santa Clara pottery, which is indistinguishable from that produced by the neighboring San Ildefonso pueblo, is an important aspect of the economy of the pueblo. Over 300 potters are active at Santa Clara. Both carved and painted polished redware and blackware are made, along with some open-fired pieces which have a brownish-black appearance. Some polychrome work is made, and the sgraffito technique—which involves shallow carving after firing—is also employed.

SANTA CLARA (sahn'-ta clar'-a) —

Spanish for Saint Claire. Native name is *Kah'P'o*, meaning "wild rose place." Language: Tewa. Reservation: 45,744 acres. Population: 1,742. Government: Officers and council elected annually by adult tribal members. Tribal constitution adopted in 1935—the first pueblo to do so. Dances: June 8 - Buffalo Dance. June 13 - San Antonio Feast Day and dances. Late July - Puye' Ruins Fiesta. Aug. 12 - Corn Dance and Feast Day. ■

According to their tradition the Tewas emerged from the underworld through Sip-ophe, a small lake in the sand dune country near Alamosa, Colorado. Before they settled in their present locations, the Tewas occupied several villages in the Ojo Caliente area in addition to the cliff dwellings at Puye'. Santa Clara, one of six Tewa-speaking pueblos in New Mexico, was built in the 14th century.

The Spaniards established a church at the village in the 1620s. The present church, which dates from 1918, occupies the site of the original structure.

At the time of the Great Pueblo Revolt the people of Santa Clara attacked a small party of Spanish soldiers at the pueblo, fortified the village against possible attack, and joined their allies to lay siege to Santa Fe. Later they joined other Tewas in the pueblo fortress atop Black Mesa. Some moved west to take up residence with the Zuni and Hopi. After the reconquest of New Mexico many moved back to reoccupy their village.

In the late 1800s, Santa Clara split into opposing factions over a controversy involving the acceptance of federal programs. Those who wished to cooperate with the government were accused of abandoning the old ways, and charges of witchcraft were common.

The adoption of a tribal constitution in 1935 did much to heal this factionalism. Today, the traditional religious hierarchy directs the ceremonial life of the village, and secular affairs are left in the hands of the progressive, educated young. The arrangement has been so successful that many of the disenfranchised young people of neighboring villages point to Santa Clara as an example of how things could be if the religious leaders of their villages would relinquish control over secular affairs.

Santa Clara, like San Ildefonso, is famous for its polished black pottery. Over 300 potters produce large numbers of bowls, jars, plates, figurines, and miniatures. Polished redware and a red polychrome are also made.

As with most pueblos, agriculture has been superseded by wage work as the most important source of income. Many people from the pueblo are employed at Los Alamos National Laboratory. Pottery making is a significant source of income for many.

Tribal income is derived from commercial property leases near Española, fishing and picnicking fees at the Santa Clara Canyon recreational area, a touring company, and admission fees charged visitors to the Puye' Ruins. A conference center has been built near Puye' which is available for non-Indian use.

SAN ILDEFONSO (san il'-deh-fon-so) —

Spanish for Saint Ildefonsus. Native name is *Po-ho-ge-Oweenge*, meaning "village where the river cuts down through." Language: Tewa. Reservation: 26,191 acres. Population: 575. Government: Governor, lieutenant governor, and council elected by adult male members of tribe. Dances: Jan. 6 - Eagle Dance. Jan. 23 - Feast Day and Buffalo-Deer Dance and Comanche Dance. June 13 - Corn Dance. Sept. 8 - Harvest Dance. ▬▬▬

According to tradition at San Ildefonso, the cliff dwellings of Mesa Verde are the ancient homes of this tribe. Around A.D. 1300 their ancestors moved into the upper Rio Grande Valley. Archaeological evidence indicates that the Indians of San Ildefonso had also occupied three villages on the Pajarito Plateau along with other Tewa-speaking groups before they settled in their present location.

The actual village site has been shifted a number of times. The village that Oñate visited in 1598 was located about one mile from the present pueblo. In the late 1800s, San Ildefonso was moved north of its old location, which meant that the kiva was no longer in the plaza. Problems that afflicted the pueblo afterwards were attributed to the move, and some years later a portion of the residents moved back to what became known as the South Plaza. The split and resultant factionalism affected both the religious and civil organization of the pueblo, with the North Plaza retaining civil authority. Since the mid-1970s, changes to the tribal council have caused the factionalism to subside.

A small pueblo, San Ildefonso not only suffered losses during the Great Pueblo Revolt and two subsequent revolts, but endured two smallpox epidemics in the late 1700s that reduced their population by more than half. An influenza epidemic in 1918 further dropped their numbers to less than 100. (During the first quarter of this century most Rio Grande pueblos had a death rate higher than their birth rate.) Wage work and craftwork are the major sources of income currently, though they also do some farming and stock raising. Tribal income is derived from fishing permits.

San Ildefonso shares a concern with other nearby pueblos over outside pollution threats to their lands, and is working with Los Alamos National Laboratory and nearby communities to resolve the problems.

There is a tribally owned lake where fishing is allowed by permit. Like most pueblos, photography is regulated and by permit only. Additionally, no early morning photography is allowed under any circumstances. There is also an admission fee to enter the pueblo.

The Comanche Dance is one of the dances that may be given at San Ildefonso Pueblo on their feast day, observed each year on January 23. It is a time when many people from surrounding pueblos come to take part in the celebration.

NAMBE (nahm-bay') — from the native word meaning "mound of earth." Language: Tewa. Reservation: 19,124 acres. Population: 630. Government: Governor and four officials elected annually by members of the pueblo. A council of past governors does the decision-making. Dances: Oct. 4 - St. Francis Day, Feast Day and dances.

The Spanish established a church in Nambe in the early 1600s. Revolts, decay, and fire destroyed each of the churches built between then and 1975, at which time the current one was constructed. There are remains of an older pueblo nearby, dating from around 1300, but there is also speculation that the current pueblo of Nambe was founded in 1598 by Tewas from other nearby pueblos. Very little is known of its history—either from Spanish records or archaeological work.

Only their kiva immediately distinguishes Nambe from other small rural settlements in the Rio Grande Valley, identifying it as an Indian community. The extensive outlines of old walls show that Nambe has declined considerably in size since its founding.

Intermarriage with the local Spanish-American population has been responsible for a weakening of tribal authority, and a gradual breakdown of traditional native life. A revival of ceremonialism—typical of a general trend in many Rio Grande pueblos during the past decade—has reversed the loss of native traditions that had caused many to predict the complete end of native culture here and at Pojoaque.

Craftwork is limited to some weaving, a little jewelry, and pottery work—some of which utilizes a micaceous clay found in the area, and the rest of which is typical Tewa red and black polished ware. Wage work—mostly off-reservation—some farming, and stock raising are the major

Traditional Tewa ceremonies had begun to disappear at Nambe Pueblo. In a reversal of this trend, the older ways have been revived to help reach a strong future.

components of the tribe's economy, along with income from recreational activities which center around Nambe Falls, a picturesque area developed by the pueblo. The tribe also owns and operates a tour company in northern New Mexico. Fees are charged for fishing, camping, picnicking, and sightseeing.

Kivas have been the heart of pueblo religious activity for over a thousand years. Beginning in the 1980s, there has been a resurgence of traditional ceremonialism among many Rio Grande pueblos.

SAN JUAN (san hwan') — Spanish for Saint

John. Native name is *Okeh*. Language: Tewa. Reservation: 12,236 acres. Population: 2,358. Government: Religious leaders of the summer and winter people alternate in selection of secular officers. Council is made up of all former *Tuuyon* or Governors. Dances: June 24 - San Juan Feast Day and Corn, Buffalo, or Comanche dances.

San Juan is the northernmost and largest of the six Tewa-speaking pueblos. It has been continuously inhabited since A.D. 1300.

Coronado's expedition visited San Juan in 1541, but the expedition's reputation preceded it—they found the pueblo abandoned and promptly plundered it. In 1598, Oñate named the village San Juan Bautista and established the first capital of New Mexico at a village just across the river from San Juan called *Yunque Owingeh Yunque* (Mockingbird Place, renamed San Gabriel by the Spanish), whose people relinquished their pueblo to the Spanish and moved over to San Juan. The hospitality of San Juan in receiving these new residents so impressed the Spaniards that they amended the name to San Juan de los Caballeros (gentlemen).

The initial period of goodwill soon gave way to feelings of discontent and hostility as the Indians experienced the harshness of Spanish rule. Suppression of native religion reached a peak in 1675 when 47 Indian leaders from a number of pueblos were convicted of practicing witchcraft and whipped. Among them was Popay, a religious leader from San Juan, who later conceived, organized, and led the Great Pueblo Revolt of 1680 which drove the Spanish colonists from the Rio Grande Valley. This was the only time that the pueblos had ever united to achieve a common goal.

Popay then attempted to purge the country of all Spanish influence and to return the pueblos to the old way of life, but he became so tyrannical in his methods that he soon lost the support of the people. The pueblos withdrew to their own village authorities, and the spirit of intertribal cooperation

The Deer Dance is part of a hunting ritual that seeks to ensure there will always be enough deer to hunt, and also honors the spirit of the deer for it is generally believed that a successful hunt requires the cooperation of the animal itself.

disappeared. This lack of unity helped make possible the reconquest by de Vargas.

San Juan was considered a major trading center, linking the two larger centers, Taos and Santa Fe. Crops, primarily corn, hay, and alfalfa, were the major source of income and employment well into the middle of the 20th century, with nearly half of their small reservation being cultivated.

Today farming has dwindled, but San Juan is expanding its economic base to provide both tribal income and employment for individual members. Current sources of tribal revenue include fishing and camping fees, a tribal arts and crafts cooperative (Oke Oweenge, begun in 1968), gas station, convenience store, restaurant, RV campground, and gaming.

The potters of San Juan Pueblo use a mica-flecked clay. The surface may then be incised, carved, or painted or slipped and polished. Stylized cloud symbols frequently grace their work. (From left) Rosita and Norman DeHerrera, Alvin Curran

TAOS (tah'-os) — from the Spanish version of a native word, *Tua-tah*, meaning "in the village." The native name for the pueblo translates as "at red willow canyon mouth." Language: Tiwa. Reservation: 95,341 acres. Population: 2,170. Government: Religious hierarchy made up of four kiva headmen and hereditary cacique who select secular officers. Dances: Jan 1 - Turtle Dance. Jan. 6 - Animal Dance. June 13 - Corn Dance. June 24 - San Juan's Day. July 25 - Corn Dance. Sept. 29 - Sundown Dance. Sept. 30 - San Geronimo Feast Day. Dec. 24 - Christmas Eve Procession. Dec. 25 - Matachines Dance. ━━━━

The northernmost pueblo, Taos reflects Plains Indian influence in the dress, customs, and physical makeup of its people. The Ute, Apache, and Comanche met here to trade meat and hides for Pueblo foodstuffs and textiles. The multistoried construction of the pueblo was originally designed for defense, with no ground-level doors or windows and a surrounding adobe wall, giving evidence that not all contacts were peaceful.

The present village was built about 1700 after the old one, located a few hundred yards to the northeast, was destroyed by fire in the 1690s. It closely duplicates the original pueblo, consisting of two house groups: *Hlauuma* (North House) and *Hlaukwima* (South House) located on either side of Taos Creek.

Alvarado first visited Taos in 1540. In 1598 Oñate, following the Spanish custom of assigning saints' names to the pueblos, named it San Miguel. No trace remains of the original mission of San Geronimo which was established in the early 17th century. The church ruins (also called San Geronimo) inside the wall date from 1706. The present church was built in 1847.

Dissatisfaction with Spanish rule led to the abandonment of the village in 1639, and the people moved onto the plains with the Jicarilla Apache. They built a new pueblo in what is now Scott County, Kansas, remaining there for two years before they were brought back to the old pueblo by the Spaniards.

Trouble with Spanish authority continued, and Taos served as the base of operations for the planners of the Great Pueblo Revolt of 1680. On August 10 of that year, Taos warriors killed the resident priests and Spanish settlers and joined the other pueblos in attacking Santa Fe. The move was a military success, and Governor Otermin was forced to flee south to El Paso with all the surviving colonists.

Taos Pueblo is divided into two house groups, one on each side of Taos Creek. It is the most-photographed of all pueblos due to heavy visitation. The constant presence of a growing number of tourists in their village—designated a World Heritage Site by the United Nations—has caused an exodus to new housing outside the pueblo.

MURRAE HAYNES

MURRAE HAYNES

Intertribal powwows are not new at Taos. For hundreds of years Taos Pueblo has been the site of intertribal trade. Being on the very edge of the Pueblo region, they had contact with the Ute, Apache, and even Plains Indian tribes like the Comanche.

In 1692, the Spaniards under de Vargas began to retake the province. An uneasy truce followed, marked by a number of small revolts and temporary abandonment of Taos when the people fled to nearby mountain canyons to escape Spanish reprisals.

The only major uprising at Taos after the United States assumed control of the territory occurred in 1847. The Taos Rebellion, instigated in part by Mexican pioneer settlers who harbored ill feelings toward the new American authorities, resulted in the deaths of Governor Charles Bent and 7 Americans. Troops from Santa Fe attacked and killed 150 rebels who sought refuge inside the church (the ruins of which are still visible) and later executed 15 more.

Encroachment on pueblo land by white squatters led to a threatened uprising in 1910, but the appearance of troops prevented bloodshed. Land-related controversies continued, however, with the most important regarding the traditional use and religious significance of Blue Lake, high on Taos Mountain.

Since the turn of the century Taos attempted to have the lake included as part of tribal lands in order to protect it. While ranchers were given ten-year grazing permits, Taos Indians were given only three days in August for exclusive use. Even then they had to notify the appropriate government agency in writing ten days in advance of their intention to hold their ancient ceremonies. The Taos people remained firm in their demand for the land—not money for the land—and the government finally capitulated.

In 1970, Taos Blue Lake was officially returned to them. (The current reservation contains less than one-third of the land they once used.)

The adoption of the peyote cult by some members in the 1890s led to 50 years of bitter factionalism within the pueblo. Factionalism over the control of village affairs and limited economic opportunities have led many younger members to leave the pueblo in search of employment and different living conditions. (Electricity and running water are not available in the oldest portions of the pueblo, which is also visited daily by large numbers of tourists. Lack of amenities and privacy have caused a number of tribal members to leave the pueblo.)

Nevertheless, Taos continues to function as a Pueblo society, held together by the strong ties of a common language, culture, and religion.

Crafts produced include drums, moccasins, jewelry, and pottery made from the distinctive mica-flecked clay found in the area. Tourist-related activities (including a casino) are the major source of tribal income. The tribe recently opened its own health clinic, and has been active in encouraging and providing for educational opportunities for tribal members. Current water-rights negotiations with the state of New Mexico may hold the key to greater self-sufficiency for this tribe.

The church at Picuris was built in the 1770s after the tribe returned from seeking refuge with the Jicarilla Apache in what is now western Kansas. The building restoration is one aspect of their economic development plans.

PICURIS (pee-kuu-rees') — probably a Spanish version of the Keresan name *Pikuria*, meaning "those who paint." Native name is *Piwwetha*, meaning "pass in the mountains." Language: Tiwa. Reservation: 14,980 acres. Population: 233. Government: Tribal officers elected by adult men. Dances: Aug. 10 - San Lorenzo Feast Day and Corn Dance.

Picuris and Taos are descended from a common ancestral group which settled in this general area about A.D. 900. Sometime during the 12th century these people split to form two separate tribes. Picuris, like Taos, has had considerable contact with Plains tribes in general and the Jicarilla Apache in particular, with whom they frequently intermarried.

The Tiwa Indians of Picuris are related to those of Taos Pueblo. Like Taos, with whom they have close ties, they produce a micaceous clay pottery. Pottery making is a craft passed down from one generation to the next within a family. (Left to right) Cora Durand, Frances Martinez, Anthony Durand

The original pueblo, now partially excavated, lies on the north edge of the present village. It dates from about A.D. 1250, and was first visited by the Spaniards in the early 1540s. They named the village San Lorenzo, and established a mission there in 1621.

Luis Tapato, one of the leaders of the Great Pueblo Revolt, was a governor of Picuris. The pueblo, which at that time had a population estimated at between 2,000 and 3,000, played an important role in the rebellion by providing a large force of fighting men for the campaign against the Spanish.

In 1692, they once again swore allegiance to Spanish authority, but followed this with three more revolts in less than five years. After the last uprising, in 1696, they abandoned their village to seek refuge at the Jicarilla Apache settlement of El Cuartelejo in western Kansas. In 1706, greatly decimated by disease and warfare, 300 people returned to their pueblo. The present church was built in the 1770s following their resettlement.

In the 1930s, traditional life at Picuris suffered as the tiny population (fewer than 100) faced a court decision that deprived them of most of their irrigated farmland. Several governors elected by the tribal council were impeached during this time—at the request of the Bureau of Indian Affairs, not tribal members. The pueblo was renamed San Lorenzo in 1947 but changed back in 1955.

Since the late 1960s, there has been a revival of traditional religious activities. Most recently, a buffalo bull provided by the Governor of Taos from that pueblo's herd, has prompted the tribe to consider building a herd of its own.

The isolation of the tiny pueblo has hindered development, forcing many to seek employment off-reservation. Fewer than half of all tribal members live on the reservation.

Two small lakes, Pu-na and Tu-tah, provide revenue from fishing and camping permits. A shop and restaurant also provide some income, as does a tribally owned hotel located in Santa Fe.

There is a fee for photography on the reservation. Crafts are limited to some jewelry and a little pottery—some of which is painted, while the rest is left with a finish created by the mica-flecked clay they use.

UTE (yoot) — from *Yuta*, the Shoshone and Comanche name for this tribe. Native name is *Nooche,* meaning "the people." Language: Shoshonean. Reservations: Southern Ute Reservation (Colorado) - 302,000 acres, Ute Mountain Reservation (Colorado and New Mexico) - 555,000 acres, and Uintah and Ouray Reservation (Utah) - 852,411 acres. Population: Southern Ute - 1,316, Ute Mountain - 1,911, and Uintah and Ouray - 3,154. Government (Southern Ute): Constitutional form of government provides for election of a six-member tribal council. ▬▬▬▬▬

Though they produce other items, such as flutes, the Ute are best-known for their buckskin and beadwork crafts. Ranching and farming, however, produce most of their income.

The Utes today occupy reservations in three states—Utah, Colorado, and New Mexico. This distribution is indicative of the tremendous area that was once claimed by the ten or more bands that make up this tribe. Their territory stretched from the Great Salt Lake southeast to the Four Corners region, and included most of Colorado and portions of northern New Mexico.

Originally these people lived in small family groups and subsisted in the manner of most Great Basin tribes—by hunting and gathering. Linguistically they are related to the Chemehuevi and Paiute. Culturally they were closely related to the Southern Paiute until they acquired horses from the Spaniards in the early 1800s. They then extended their hunting range onto the buffalo plains where they picked up traits typical of the Plains Indian cultures. This new mobility also allowed the family groups to unite into bands as political and social units. A single Ute "tribe" did not exist although bands might occasionally join forces to meet a common enemy.

The Ute maintained friendly relations with the Jicarilla Apache, Shoshone, and Paiute; traded with the northern Rio Grande Pueblos; and warred with the Navajo, Kiowa, Cheyenne, Comanche, and Sioux. At one time they even joined with the Spanish in a temporary alliance against the Comanche.

Although contact with Europeans began in 1776 with a visit from Father Escalante, the Ute felt little effect from white contact until the mid-1800s when American settlers began to arrive.

From 1849 through the end of the 1800s, the Americans made and broke a series of treaties with the Ute. After Colorado became a state in 1876, a public clamor was raised to remove the Ute in order to provide more land for settlers. Each demand resulted in a new treaty and less land for the Ute until one chief was led to sarcastically ask if the U.S. lacked the power to enforce its own treaties. (The land originally allotted to the Ute in 1868 was about 16,000,000 acres—it was reduced by more than 14,000,000 acres in less

than 30 years.) That the displacement of the Ute took place with a minimum of bloodshed is a tribute to Ouray, a leader of the Southern Utes, who recognized the futility of warring against overwhelming odds.

With the loss of their best hunting grounds, the Ute became dependent upon government rations during their early reservation years.

Today the Southern Utes, made up of the Weeminuche, Capote, and Moache bands, occupy two reservations in southwestern Colorado and a small part of New Mexico. Farming, stock raising, and sheepherding provide their main livelihood. Tribal income from gas and oil leases, gaming, and money obtained from a land claim settlement with the U.S. government is being used to develop and improve rangelands and purchase off-reservation ranches to better the economic standard of the people.

Little remains of the native culture—the Bear Dance, an annual spring ceremony, and the Sun Dance (derived from the Plains tribes) are still held, but are regarded by many as more of a social occasion than a religious one. A number of Ute Mountain groups are members of the Native American Church.

Crafts are becoming increasingly scarce, but beaded buckskin bags, belts, and moccasins are still being made along with some coiled basketry and hand-painted greenware pottery.

ZUNI (zoo'-nee) — Spanish pronunciation of the Keresan name for this pueblo, *Sunyi*. The Zuni name for themselves is *A:shiwi*. Language: Zunian. Reservation: 421,481 acres, including a 10,085 - acre religious site in Arizona. Population: 8,996. Government: Tribal officers elected biennially by adult members. Dances: Late November or early December - Shalako. Spring and summer months - Kokko (katsina) dances. ▬

The Zuni are the best-known fetish carvers, but other tribes make them as well—and in increasing numbers. Represented here are Zuni, Hualapai, Navajo, and Santa Clara artists.

Archaeological evidence indicates that the distinctive culture of the Zuni is the result of a blending of at least two diverse cultural groups in prehistoric times. This "melting pot" situation continued well into historic times as the Zuni absorbed into their population Indians from other areas, including a number of Tlascalans from central Mexico who had formed a part of Coronado's expedition. Linguistically, Zuni is unrelated to any other tribe in the Southwest.

At the beginning of the historic period the Zuni, numbering well over 3,000, occupied six villages in the broad Zuni Valley—the largest of these was Hawikuh. The present pueblo is built on the old site of Halona, one of the original towns that made up the province of Shiwona.

In 1529, Fray Marcos de Niza set out from Mexico to determine if this settlement could be the fabled Seven Cities of Cibola, which reportedly held the treasure of Montezuma. His advance scouting party was led by Estevan, a Moorish slave who had explored the Gulf of Mexico and Texas with Cabeza de Vaca. Estevan's earlier successes in dealing with Indian tribes failed him at Zuni. The Indians found his lordly attitude offensive, and cured his bad manners by killing him shortly after he reached Hawikuh and began making demands upon the people.

After receiving news of Estevan's death, de Niza traveled only far enough to get a glimpse of Hawikuh before retracing his steps to Mexico. There, in a report unbecoming a man of the cloth, he announced that he had found the Kingdom of Cibola.

The following year Francisco Coronado mounted an expedition to Zuni. He attacked and captured Hawikuh only to discover that de Niza's glowing report was a hoax.

The Franciscans built a mission at Hawikuh in 1629. The presence of the missionaries caused dissension among the Zuni and resulted in the death of two friars in 1632. Three Zunis then fled to a fortified village on Dowa Yalane (Corn Mountain), a mesa southeast of Zuni.

The Zuni outwardly appeared to accept Spanish rule, but actually followed a course of

A number of Zuni katsinas have been adopted and adapted by the Hopi. These Wakashi kokko appear in a very similar form at Hopi where they are known as Wakas katsinas. Sullivan Shebola

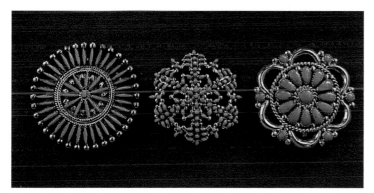

The Zuni have been working silver since the late 1800s. The techniques we now think of as typically Zuni began to develop about 1930. Styles continue to evolve, but still have their roots in the prehistoric tradition of stone and shell mosaic work.

These figurines represent dancers in the Zuni Shalako ceremony. This ceremony, held in early winter, is usually thought of as a house-blessing ceremony, but is actually a 49-day ritual re-creation of Zuni emergence and migration legends. Called katsinas by the Hopi, the Zuni name for these figures is kokko. While carving such figures is common at Hopi, it is infrequent at Zuni.

passive (and sometimes not so passive) resistance to this new authority.

Apache raids increased in intensity during the late 1600s, and finally led to the abandonment of Hawikuh in 1672.

The Zuni supported the Great Pueblo Revolt of 1680, but were less involved in it because they were remote from the Spanish settlements. Once again they retreated to Corn Mountain and remained there until 1692, when de Vargas persuaded them to return to the valley and resettle Halona. A new church was built in the village in 1699. (It was abandoned in the early 1800s.)

Because of its prosperous appearance, Zuni gives the impression of being a very "progressive" pueblo. However, it maintains much of its traditional life, especially its religious activities. Perhaps the best known and most spectacular of its many ceremonies is the Shalako, a house-blessing ritual that occurs in November or December. It includes huge, bird-like figures called Shalakos, who are the couriers of the rainmakers.

Subsistence farming and stock raising, supplemented by wage work, some seasonal employment (such as fire fighting), and jewelry making form the economic base of the tribe. Over 1,000 silversmiths, stonecutters, and fetish carvers work full or part time at their craft. Pottery making has been revived in recent years, but weaving and basketry have disappeared.

NAVAJO (nah'-vah-ho) —from a Tewa word

Navahu, meaning "cultivated fields." (Also spelled Navaho, though Navajo has been adopted as the preferred spelling by the tribal government.) Native name *Dine'* (din-neh') means "the people." Language: Athabascan. Reservations: Navajo, Alamo, Canoncito, and Ramah totaling 17,500,815 acres. Population: 219,198. Government: Constitution adopted in 1938 provides for tribal council delegates elected by adult members of the tribe. Headed by a chair and vice-chair elected at large.

The common ancestors of the Navajo and Apache reached the northernmost fringes of the Southwest some time after A.D. 1200 as small nomadic bands of hunters and gatherers. Linguistically, they are related to the Athabascan-speaking tribes of northwestern Canada. The way of life of each band was modified by its contact with other tribes. The Navajo were particularly influenced by the Pueblo Indians—weaving, agriculture, sandpainting, and certain ceremonial rituals were some of the customs they are believed to have adopted. As agriculture grew in economic importance, the Navajo became less nomadic and began to settle in small communities near their fields.

A Spanish reference to "Apaches de Navajo" (generally regarded as being a composite Pueblo name meaning "enemies of the cultivated fields") as a semi-sedentary agricultural people appears in 1626. It is the first mention of the Navajo that distinguished them from the Apache. Contact with the Spanish had far-reaching effects on both the Navajo and the Spaniards. With the acquisition of sheep and goats, the Indians began to lead a life that was more pastoral than agricultural.

Monument Valley, near the northern edge of the Navajo Reservation, is known the world over for its scenic beauty, often featured in movies. Called Tse'Bii'Nidzisgai— Plain Rocks—by the Navajo, it is a hard land in which to make a living, supporting only five people per square mile.

The use of the horse allowed them to increase their raiding activities, much to the sorrow of Indian and Spanish communities along the Rio Grande Valley. (They expanded westward as well, forcing the Havasupai out of the Little Colorado River region by 1686.) The Navajo considered their forays not as war but as an economic pursuit that yielded livestock, food, booty, women, and slaves. (The great use of Indian slaves by the Spanish probably stimulated this practice.) For this reason the Navajo were never as interested in driving the Spanish out of the Southwest as were the Pueblo tribes.

In 1745, the Franciscans made an attempt to establish missions among the Navajo of the Mount Taylor region. After two years the Indians rejected the new religion, but remained friendly to the Spanish. Because of this peaceful coexistence the Navajo of Canoncito and Alamo are still sometimes known by their fellow tribesmen by an old name meaning "the people who are enemies."

When the Americans assumed jurisdiction of New Mexico in 1846, they sought to control the

Football games on an irrigated field in the arid Monument Valley are a measure of the influence non-Navajo culture and technology are beginning to have on Navajos. The Navajo have thus far managed to adapt elements from other cultures without losing their own identity.

Navajo pictographs often portray actual historical events. This one records a raid by Utes in Navajo country in January, 1858.

RALPH LEE HOPKINS

The Navajo have moved back into Canyon de Chelly and rebuilt the homes, fields, and orchards that were destroyed during the scorched earth campaign led by Kit Carson in 1863.

GAIL BANDINI

Navajo by establishing military posts in their country. Without understanding the political makeup of the tribe, the U.S. military signed peace treaties with several "chiefs." The chiefs were actually merely headmen whose authority did not extend beyond their own small bands. Naturally, raiding by other bands continued since they had not been a part of the negotiations.

In 1863, Navajo depredations became so serious that a military force under Kit Carson was dispatched to subdue the tribe. Carson accomplished this objective not through military engagements, but by wiping out the economic basis of Navajo life. Livestock was slaughtered, crops and fruit trees were destroyed, and hogans were leveled.

By March of 1864, 2,400 Navajos had been rounded up to begin the 300-mile journey to their place of confinement at Fort Sumner on the Pecos River in southeastern New Mexico. Eventually some 8,000 men, women, and children made "The Long Walk" to captivity. An estimated 1,800 avoided capture by hiding out in the more inaccessible areas of their country.

Conditions at the Bosque Redondo reservation were miserable. Drought problems were aggravated by government contractors who cheated the Navajos out of much of their food

Trading posts were the first contact points between Navajos and the American government, which claimed jurisdiction over the various sovereign Navajo bands. While Americans often found the customs of the Navajo puzzling and odd, the actions of the American government were every bit as strange and puzzling to the Navajo. One of the services traders often provided was to try and explain the new laws and regulations. The early trading post acted as a bank, post office, meeting place, livestock buyer, and general store. Redwing Nez

and supplies, and what was sent was generally of inferior quality. More than 2,000 Navajos died from disease before the government decided the relocation plan was a failure.

In 1868, the Navajos were allowed to return home. Sadly, this move was prompted not so much by humanitarian motives as by economic motives—it would be cheaper to allow them to become self-supporting in their homeland than to support them in confinement. But their troubles were not over—the white man had not yet lost his taste for Indian land, and clashes occurred. The schools promised in the treaty of 1868 were run like reformatories, and did much to maintain a hostile attitude toward whites.

Despite these problems the Navajo did make a comeback and became self-sufficient. Sheep and cattle became the basis of the Navajo economy, and a lively trade was maintained in wool and hides. Navajo weaving and silver found ready markets. The Navajo prospered, and their flocks of sheep increased to more than 300,000 by 1878.

By the 1930s, the basis of Navajo life, sheep, had increased to the point where the land was seriously overgrazed—erosion had become a major problem and land productivity plummeted. Sheep herds had grown to over 1,000,000 by 1933, leaving only one possible solution—drastic stock reduction. This was another critical blow to Navajo life, and the controversial manner in which it was administered is still bitterly remembered.

Navajo hogans or homes are low, round buildings built with whatever materials are available in that area of Navajoland. The doorway always faces east, a custom observed even in many modern Navajo homes.

Despite its size (roughly the area of West Virginia) the reservation has limited resources and much of the land, however scenic, is virtually worthless from the standpoint of economic development. Thousands of Navajos leave the reservation to seek employment. Craftwork, while providing an income, primarily for silver-

The Navajo suffered greatly at the hands of the U.S. military under the scorched earth campaign conducted to force them from their homes—lands they were returned to when the relocation effort failed. Yet even given that history, and incidents like the stock reductions of the 1930s that impoverished many Navajo, when the U.S. was attacked December 7, 1941, Navajo young men joined their counterparts across the country in signing up for military service. The Navajo Codetalkers, using a code developed in their own language, were instrumental in helping defeat the Japanese military, which was never able to break the code. U.S. military service continues to be a source of pride among the Navajo, and a special memorial to Navajo veterans was established at Window Rock in 1995.

Raising livestock is a major source of income for many Navajo families and has been since the Spanish introduced sheep, goats, horses, and cattle to the Southwest over 300 years ago.
Shirley Rockwell

smiths, is of minor importance in the overall economy.

The first Navajo council began with three Navajos, hand-picked by the Secretary of the Interior, and its first meeting was held for the purpose of ratifying gas and oil leases in a rapidly declining market.

Considerable tribal income is currently derived from gas, oil, and coal leases. Much of this income is being invested in tribal enterprises which in turn are providing jobs for Indians on the reservation. Not all of these ventures have been economically or environmentally sound, causing some—notably the tribal lumber industry—to

People who played cowboys and Indians as children probably never realized that sometimes cowboys are Indians or vice versa. The Navajo have their own rodeo circuit, and many belong to the national American Indian Rodeo Cowboy Association.

Navajo culture seems to be able to absorb many outside influences without losing its identity. A Pioneer Day parade at Navajo Mountain led by a baton-twirling majorette is still an unmistakably Navajo event. At the head of the parade, in a position of honor, are the Navajo elders in traditional dress.

Work by Navajo painters has been avidly collected for three quarters of a century. While non-Navajo art critics argue about what is traditional or authentically Indian in paintings, Navajos continue to develop their own visions and styles. Shonto Begay

come under fire from tribal members. Serious problems still face the tribe, but for the Navajo adversity has long been a constant condition.

A long-simmering land use conflict with the Hopi, which resulted in additions to the Navajo reservation from land originally set aside for the Hopi and a declaration of a Joint Use Area, is still a sensitive issue. Aggravated by the need to clear title for a coal mining lease (and by subsequent water problems), the land was partitioned in 1974, with both Hopi and Navajo relocations required. The Navajo tribe received 400,000 acres to accommodate the relocatees, but some have chosen to remain.

A historic agreement between the tribes, mediated by the federal government in 1992, promised to finally resolve the issue. It was undermined by the non-Indian majority of the state of Arizona, so the problem remains unresolved into the second century of its existence.

The tribe, in addition to forming an economic development authority, has built hospitals, airports, a museum and zoo, and an accredited tribal community college system, and is planning a resort. They voted down gaming in 1995. Unemployment is estimated to be roughly 30 percent.

Indian reservation boundary markers are almost never carved in stone anymore—and with good reason. Rare is the tribe that has not had its boundaries changed at least a couple of times since their reservation was established. The Navajo Reservation boundary has been changed nearly 50 times since it was established in 1868.

NEVADA

UTAH

ARIZONA

PAIUTE

Las Vegas

NAVAJO

NAVAJO

Colorado River

HAVASUPAI

HOPI

NAVAJO

HUALAPAI

Navajo

MOHAVE

HUALAPAI

Flagstaff

Colorado River

CHEMEHUEVI

Bill Williams River

YAVAPAI & APACHE

ZUNI

Mohave

CALIFORNIA

Colorado River Reservation (NAVAJO, HOPI, MOHAVE & CHEMEHUEVI)

WHITE MOUNTAIN APACHE

Chemehuevi

YAVAPAI & APACHE

Salt River

Phoenix

SAN CARLOS APACHE

YUMA

Gila River

PIMA & MARICOPA

PIMA

Western Apache

COCOPA

TOHONO O'ODHAM

YAQUI

Tucson

TOHONO O'ODHAM

TOHONO O'ODHAM

Tohono O'odham

Tohono O'odham

UTE

UTE

NAVAJO

COLORADO

NEW MEXICO

JICARILLA
APACHE

Rio Chama

TAOS

PICURIS

San Juan

SAN JUAN
POJOAQUE
SANTA CLARA
SAN ILDEFONSO
NAMBE
TESUQUE
JEMEZ
● *Santa Fe*
COCHITI
● *Gallup*
ZIA
SANTO DOMINGO
SAN FELIPE
SANTA ANA
SANDIA
RAMAH-NAVAJO
ACOMA
● *Albuquerque*
ZUNI
CANONCITO-NAVAJO
ISLETA
Zuni
LAGUNA

ALAMO-NAVAJO

Rio Grande

MESCALERO
APACHE

Jicarilla
Apache

Jicarilla
Apache

INDIAN RESERVATIONS
OF THE SOUTHWEST

Each tribe in the Southwest has its own distinct traditions which have evolved over time. The clothing they wear has also evolved over time and reflects the climate, way of life, and their beliefs, as well as influences from other groups—Indian and non-Indian. As examples: Some of the northern Pueblo tribes have forms of dress borrowed from the westernmost Plains tribes, while the current "traditional" style of dress among the Navajo was influenced by Anglo fashions from the post-Civil War era.

environment. Tiny springs at the mesa edge, fed by the drainage of Black Mesa, have sustained the villages for centuries. Because of their expertness at dry farming they have been able to grow crops of corn, squash, beans, and cotton on land that would give nightmares to a Midwestern farmer.

A short growing season (133 days) and limited rainfall (12 inches per year) made it imperative to obtain the help of supernatural forces to ensure adequate moisture and bountiful harvests. It was only natural that this would be the focus of Hopi religious activities. Much time was spent in performing complex and beautiful rituals designed

The katsina— here emerging from a kiva— plays a major role in Hopi life.

Corn is still important at Hopi, where it may be prepared in countless ways—boiled, parched, baked, and roasted—or even ground for use as a prayer offering.

HOPI (hoe'-pih) — a contraction of *Hopituh*, their tribal name, which is generally translated as "the peaceful ones." Language: Shoshonean. Reservation: 1,561,213 acres. Population: 9,199. Government: Constitution adopted 1936. Hopi tribal council made up of 15 members, most of whom are elected by villages according to population, but several are appointed by the *kikmongwi* (priest-chief) of their village. Chair and vice-chair are elected at large. Ceremonials: Katsina dances performed from January until late July. Unmasked dances begin in August and continue through December. ▬▬▬▬▬

Hopi tradition tells of the people inhabiting three underworlds before emerging into the present world. The settlement of land is explained in terms of individual clans who wandered about and occupied many sites prior to settling in their present villages. There is no doubt that the Hopi tribe is made up of numerous groups of diverse origins.

At first appearance the arid mesa country of the Hopi appears incapable of supporting a permanent population. Yet, this agricultural tribe has not only existed but often thrived in a hostile

to bring about the desired results. Today, the Hopi still maintain one of the most active religious calendars of the Southwestern tribes.

At the time of the Spanish contact in 1540, the Hopi occupied seven independent villages. The Hopi submitted to Spanish rule after Pedro de Tovar attacked and defeated the pueblo of Kawaikuh. Oñate, in 1598, received formal promises of loyalty from the Hopi, but because they remained on the Spanish frontier no civil authority was established among them, nor were they required to pay tribute to the Crown.

Walpi, founded over 300 years ago, was moved to its current site to protect the village from Spanish attack. The narrow path leading to the village has also protected it from the onslaught of modern technology. This village still does without electricity or running water, a fact of life viewed by the residents with mixed emotions. Bottled gas is generally used for lighting and cooking, while wood and coal-fired stoves are the primary source of heat. Without power poles to give it away, at a distance the village blends with the rocky mesa.

The Hopi were subjected to missionary activities in the 1600s when the Franciscans established missions in several of the villages, but Spanish influence was much less intensive than among the Rio Grande pueblos. New crops, fruit trees, livestock, and metal tools were acquired, but religious and political life were virtually untouched. The Spanish system of selecting governors for secular offices was never adopted.

Nevertheless, the Hopi were anxious to rid themselves of any Spanish control, and joined the eastern pueblos in the Great Pueblo Revolt of

Hopi weaving is done by the men, who also embroider the kilts, sashes, belts, leggings, mantas, and shirts used in their religious ceremonies. Because there are few Hopi weavers today, many Hopi have to trade for woven goods with other pueblos—or improvise. In the home of Joe and Janice Day

1680. Resident Spanish priests were killed and the missions destroyed, and the Hopi remained hostile to all subsequent attempts to reestablish Spanish authority. Awatobi, which was friendly to the Spanish and their priests, was attacked and destroyed by warriors from the other Hopi pueblos and the survivors absorbed into the villages of the attackers.

Hopis maintained friendly relations with most tribes, and traveled great distances to trade with other people. (Hopi weaving is still much sought after by the Rio Grande pueblos.) Occasionally, in times of drought, they left their villages to take up temporary residence with the Havasupai or Zuni. The Navajo and Ute, who harassed the Hopi with their constant raiding, were regarded as traditional enemies.

During some ceremonies, children not yet initiated into the Katsina Society are given katsina dolls that they are told have been carved for them by the katsinas themselves. Sidney Talas

Hopi overlay jewelry, first developed in the 1930s, involves cutting the design out of one sheet of silver and overlaying it on a second, solid sheet.

The first Hopi-owned and operated store opened in the 1930s. The Hopi Cooperative Arts and Crafts Guild formed shortly after World War II. In recent years, a number of Hopi—many of them artists—have opened their own shops and galleries. Currently there are more than a dozen Hopi-owned and operated enterprises on the reservation. Shops like Tsakurshovi provide visitors and collectors with an opportunity to meet some of the artists whose work they prize.

Hopi pottery comes in many forms and styles, but the polychrome ware produced at the villages on First Mesa (Hano, Sichomovi, and Walpi) is the best-known. Nona Naha

Anglo contact, which began in 1826, has had a much greater effect on Hopi life. Policies of the Bureau of Indian Affairs and the influence of Christian missionaries have resulted in considerable factionalism among the Hopi villages and disruption of their way of life. Nevertheless, it is apparent that the Hopi have retained much of their native culture.

Not all villages completely accept the authority of the Hopi tribal council—established in its present form in 1951—recognizing instead the traditional form of village government which accepts the *kikmongwi* (village priest-chief) as the authority. Much factionalism has resulted from the insistence of the U.S. government that the Hopi be dealt with as a single tribe rather than as separate autonomous pueblos in the manner of the Rio Grande pueblos.

Mining leases for the coal on Black Mesa provide some income (early estimates were that the state of Arizona was collecting more in related taxes than the Hopi and Navajo combined were receiving in royalties), and enormous problems. The need for clear title to the land in order to contract with a mining company sharpened the long unresolved and festering dispute over land assigned originally to the Hopi and then later designated for use (and occupied) by both Hopi and Navajo. (In a remarkable deviation from normal legal procedures, the BIA approved

a contract with a firm that represented both the Hopi and the mining company.)

Farming and stock raising are still important economic pursuits among the Hopi, although they are jeopardized by a plummeting water table (causing important and sacred springs to dry up) which many blame on the daily pumping of several million gallons of water needed for the mining operation at Black Mesa.

Wage work provides the bulk of individual income. Gaming was proposed as a source of revenue, but tribal members decisively voted it down. In recent years craftwork has provided a growing source of earnings for many individuals. No other tribe produces a greater variety of crafts than the Hopi—pottery, katsinas, silverwork, weaving, and three types of basketry.

Hopi dances, certainly as beautiful and impressive as any in the world, are dramatized prayers for rain, the growth of crops, renewal of the cycle of life, and the health and well-being of not only the Hopi but all people and all living beings. Unlike the Rio Grande pueblos, Hopi dances—both masked and unmasked—were usually open to the public, but repeated attempts by individuals to photograph and videotape religious observances in open violation of Hopi law has caused many villages to close their ceremonies to non-Hopi in recent years.

First Mesa

WALPI (wal'-pih) — "place of the gap." The people of Walpi occupied two earlier sites on the lower terrace of First Mesa before moving to their present location in 1680. Fear of a Spanish reprisal for their part in the Great Pueblo Revolt prompted them to change to a more defensive position. The move worked well, for neither of two punitive expeditions sent by the Spanish attacked the village because of its impregnable appearance.

POLACCA (po-lah'-kah) — This community at the foot of the mesa was settled in the late 1800s by First Mesa people who wished to live near the trading post and day school.

SICHOMOVI (si-cho'-mo-vee) — meaning "place of the mound where wild currants grow"—was founded about 1750 as a colony of Walpi. It is also referred to as "Middle Village" because it is flanked by Walpi and Hano.

MARK BAHTI

Hopi pottery styles continue to evolve as potters experiment with different clays, forms, and styles. Some styles are inspired by other Pueblo pottery or prehistoric forms—like the melon bowl in this group. Alton Konalestewa

Looking across Hopiland to the Second Mesa villages of Shipaulovi and Mishongnovi, one can better see the rock formations referred to as mesas—from the Spanish word for table. First, Second, and Third Mesa received their rather dull names from Anglo visitors who named them in the order they found them.

Nuva'tukya'ovi—Snow Mountain. Known to non-Hopi as the San Francisco Peaks, they are sacred to the Hopi, whose katsina spirits are believed to inhabit their highest reaches. In a losing battle, the Hopi and the Navajo—who also revere them as a sacred place—have sought to keep skiers and mountain climbers from reaching and possibly desecrating those high sacred places. At the base of the mountains lie several ancestral villages of the Hopi.

HANO (hah'-no) — The Hopi name for this Tewa village may be derived from *anopi* which means "eastern people" or it may be a mispronunciation of the Spanish name for the Tewas, which was *Los Tanos*. (A popular Hopi story claims Hano is a nickname derived from the frequent use of the syllable "ha" in Tewa speech.) Hano was settled by Tewa refugees from the Rio Grande Valley after the Great Pueblo Revolt. The Hopi claim the Tewa sought refuge from the Spanish, while the Tewa claim the Hopi asked them to help protect Walpi. The argument is as old as the village. Despite their long association with the Hopi, the Tewa people retain their own language and religious customs. Nampeyo, the potter credited with the revival of Hopi pottery beginning in 1890, was a Tewa from Hano.

Second Mesa

SHUNGOPAVY (pronounced in Hopi: Tsi-mo'-pah-vee)—"place by the spring where the tall reeds grow"—is the most important of the villages on Second Mesa. Two earlier pueblos were located at the base of the mesa near Gray Spring. The Franciscan mission of San Bartolome was built at Old Shungopavy in 1629. It was destroyed during the 1680 revolt, and the village was abandoned in favor of the present mesa-top location.

MISHONGNOVI (mih-shong'-no-vee) — "Mishong's place"—named for Mishong, the leader of the Crow Clan, who brought his people to Hopi from the San Francisco Peaks region in A.D. 1200. The people of Shungopavy allowed them to settle at Corn Rock, a Shungopavy

OWEN SEUMPTEWA

shrine, with the understanding that they would protect it against the First Mesa people. In 1629, the Franciscans built the chapel of San Buenaventura at Mishongnovi. It was destroyed and the village abandoned in 1680. The present pueblo was established shortly thereafter.

SHIPAULOVI (shih-pau'-lo-vee) — "the mosquitoes"—was, according to tradition, settled by people from Homolovi, a prehistoric pueblo on the Little Colorado River (near the present-day town of Winslow) which they say was abandoned because of the swarms of mosquitoes that infested the area. A more likely explanation is that Shipaulovi was established after the Great Pueblo Revolt by people from Shungopavy so that in the event that the Spaniards returned and destroyed their village, Shipaulovi would be able to carry on its ceremonies and religious traditions.

Third Mesa

ORAIBI (o-rye'-bih) — "place of Orai rock"— claims (along with Acoma) to be the oldest continually inhabited town in the United States. It dates from about A.D. 1150. According to tradition, Oraibi was founded by a dissident group from Old Shungopavy. In 1629, the mission of San Francisco was established at Oraibi—the ruins of this church are north of the village. An abandoned Mennonite church, struck by lightning, stands on the mesa edge. Oraibi, with a population of 1,200, was the largest Hopi village until 1906 when a split occurred over ceremonial prerogatives, and whether or not to comply with the Bureau of Indian Affairs' policies. The problem was settled bloodlessly with a "push of war." The losers, led by Yukioma, left Oraibi and built a new village, Hotevilla. An inscription that commemorates the Oraibi split is carved into the bedrock north of the village. It reads: *Well, it have to be this way now, that when you pass me over this line it will "be done." Sept. 8th, 1906.* The clan symbols of the two leaders are included.

KYKOTSMOVI (kee-kots'-mo-vee) — "place of the hills of ruins" (also called Lower Oraibi or New Oraibi)—was settled in 1890 by people from Oraibi who wanted to live near the school and trading post. It is also the site of most Hopi tribal government offices.

The Hopi are expert dry farmers. Hopi men often had to travel considerable distances to suitable sites for planting. The village of Moencopi began as a farming outpost of Oraibi village over 40 miles to the southeast. At the very edge of the current boundary for Hopiland, it is the most reliable source of water on the reservation.

OWEN SEUMPTEWA

Factionalism within villages is probably nothing new. In 1906 push literally came to shove as two competing factions found a bloodless way to end their feuding. Two groups—one friendly to the Americans and their new ways, the other opposed to them—agreed to a "push of war." The conservative element lost and had to vacate the village in the weeks before what proved to be a bitter winter.

Though conventional housing is being built below the mesas, stone homes are still built and maintained on the mesas. The Hopi tribe has taken steps to preserve traditional stone masonry skills.

HOTEVILLA (hote'-vil-lah) — "skinned back"—derives its name from a village spring which is located in the back of a cave with a low overhang. The village was settled in 1906 by the conservative faction from Oraibi. Hotevilla has a long history of non-cooperation with the federal government, and is still regarded as the most conservative Hopi village.

BAKAVI (bah'-kah-vee) — "place of the reeds"—was settled in 1907 by a group who left the newly founded village of Hotevilla and attempted to return to Oraibi. They were refused admittance so they established their own village rather than return to Hotevilla.

MOENCOPI (mun'-ko-pih) — "place of running water"—is the westernmost of the Hopi villages. It was originally a farming settlement of Oraibi, but was established as a separate village in the 1870s by Tuvi, an Oraibi leader. Because its traditions are related to Oraibi, it is included here as a Third Mesa village even though it is located over 40 miles to the northwest. Moencopi is the only Hopi village with irrigated fields. Factionalism is beginning to result in a split, with some residents considering themselves members of either Upper Moencopi or Lower Moencopi.

APACHE (ah-pah'-chee) — from the Zuni name *Apachu*, meaning "enemy," a name they used for the Navajo. Native name varies with each band, but is usually a variation of *Nde*, *Indeh* or *Tinneh*, meaning "the people." *Inde'* (pronounced in-deh') is the most widely accepted. Language: Athabascan — related linguistically to the Athabascan tribes in Canada. (For reservations and populations, see individual listings.) ▬▬▬▬

The Apache still regularly hold Nah'ih'es—coming-of-age ceremonies—for their daughters. It is a time when the entire community gathers together.

KENJI KAWANO

The Apache, an Athabascan people, were comprised of many independent bands. They were hunters, warriors, and raiders who entered the Southwest sometime after A.D. 1200, and spread into northern Mexico by the 1500s. At the time of Spanish contact the division into separate tribal groups was still taking place. The name Apache was applied to all of these people, and is still used today as a general term for the individual tribes or bands.

Although contact with other tribes modified the culture of each group, they all remained largely dependent on hunting and gathering for subsistence. What could not be obtained by hunting, gathering, and some farming was stolen in raids on the villages of agricultural tribes.

With the acquisition of horses the range and frequency of their depredations increased until the raiding of Indian, Spanish and, later, Mexican and American settlements became a way of life. The Apaches ranged over an area that extended from southern Colorado to northern Mexico, and from central Arizona to western Texas.

Numerous unsuccessful attempts were made by the Spaniards, Mexicans, and Americans to eliminate the Apache. Military campaigns were launched against them, bounties were paid for scalps, captives were kept as slaves, and treacheries of the worst kind were perpetrated in ruthless efforts to put an end to the Apache raiders. (Because the history of this period is largely recorded by non-Apaches, the

The Gaan *or Mountain Spirit Dancers of the Apache appear during the Nah'ih'es ceremony. During this four-day celebration, the young woman coming of age is believed to have the power to bring rain and even heal with her touch. But the Gaan have other responsibilities as well. The Apache, like most tribes, mark their boundaries by sacred mountains. Those mountains and all the other mountains of their home are sacred to them and protect the Apache people. The spirits of those mountains are the Gaan. Oliver Enjady*

atrocities committed by the Apache are better known than those committed against them.) But the Apache refused to die or surrender—what they lacked in numbers they made up in ferocity and cunning. As guerrilla fighters the Apaches were unparalleled.

After the Civil War, attempts were made to confine the tribes to reservations so that the settlement of the Southwest by Anglos could proceed. Problems continued as corrupt officials cheated the Indians out of promised rations, and turned over large areas of Indian land to Anglos for mining and agricultural development. Distrust and discontent resulted and new uprisings occurred.

The last outbreak was led by Geronimo. His small band of Chiricahua renegades terrorized

Arizona, New Mexico, and northern Mexico from 1884 until their surrender in 1886. This ended the Apache wars, but not the mistreatment. The renegades were sent to Florida as prisoners of war as were *all* the Chiricahuas, men, women, and children, who had remained peaceably on the reservation—even the Apache scouts who had aided the U.S. Army in Geronimo's capture!

They were kept imprisoned far longer than any other POWs in American history—28 years. After their release in 1914 they were allowed to go home, but no land was set aside for them in their traditional homeland. Most settled on the Mescalero Reservation. Those that chose to remain in Oklahoma are known as the Fort Sill

The Apache one-string violin, crafted from an agave stalk, is still made and played by a few Apache musicians.

An Apache war cap, by Ron Preston, decorated with owl feathers in hopes the wearer would be as silent and swift as the owl. These were worn in dances and only rarely on actual raids.

Apache. Just over 100 members live on 3,568 acres of allotted land. They are distinct from the much larger Oklahoma Apache tribe, the Kiowa-Apache, a group who prefer to be known as the Plains Apache.

Western Apache

The Athabascan group known as the Western Apache originally consisted of a number of independent subtribes. The present San Carlos and White Mountain "tribes" are comprised of a number of early bands: the Mogollon, Pinaleno, Tonto, Aravaipa, Coyotero, and Chiricahua are represented in the San Carlos division, and the White Mountain "tribe" is made up of members of the Mimbreno, Mogollon, Pinaleno, Chiricahua, and Aravaipa bands.

SAN CARLOS — Reservation: 1,826,641 acres. Population: 10,120. Government: Constitution adopted 1936. Tribal corporate charter 1940. Tribal council consists of seven members elected at large, with chair and vice-chair. ∎

WHITE MOUNTAIN — Reservation: 1,686,872 acres. Population: 10,147. Government: Constitution adopted 1938. Ten-member council elected at large, with chair and vice-chair. ∎

CAMP VERDE (shared with Yavapai) — Reservation: 640 acres. Population: 650 (total). ∎

TONTO — Reservation: 85 acres. Population: 92. ∎

FORT MCDOWELL (shared with Mohave and Yavapai) — Reservation: 24,680 acres. Population: 816 (total). ∎

The nomadic bands of hunters who were to be later known as the Apache settled in what is now southwestern New Mexico, northern Mexico, and southeastern Arizona during the 1400s and early 1500s.

By the latter part of the 16th century, they had begun to raid Spanish settlements in northern Sonora and Chihuahua. Early Spanish accounts do not refer to these people as Apaches, but it is possible that the raiders, whom they called

Sumas, Jocomes, and Janos were either these Athabascan-speaking bands or were later absorbed by the Apache (probably the Chiricahua and Mimbreno Apache). After 1700 they are referred to merely as Apaches.

Attempts to missionize these people ended in a full-scale rebellion in 1684. To protect their settlements from renewed Apache attacks the Spanish established a line of presidios or fortified outposts across northern Mexico, but the tactic proved useless against the hit-and-run warfare of the Apache. Besides, the Indians were not interested in driving out the Spaniards, but merely in raiding them for horses, cattle, and booty. Expeditions against the Apaches in their own territory were equally unsuccessful since pitched battles were avoided by the Indians whenever possible.

Warfare became more intense and widespread as bands pillaged as far south as Hermosillo, Sonora, and west into Tohono O'odham country past present-day Tucson. In 1848, Tubac was abandoned along with many other settlements, and the Mexicans were pushed south. The Apaches were in control.

Conflicts with Americans began in the 1820s when beaver trappers, bounty hunters, and prospectors began to invade the Apache domain. Nevertheless, many of the Apache groups seemed interested in maintaining peaceful relations with the Americans when the U.S. assumed control of Apache country in 1853. Exactly how the Americans could lay claim to Apache territory simply because they had defeated the Mexicans mystified the Apaches—after all, neither the Spaniards nor the Mexicans had ever succeeded in defeating the Apache. The greatest problem, however, resulted from the Americans' insistence that the Indians cease raiding the Mexican settlements across the border.

Attempts to confine the Apache to reservations were largely unsuccessful because of the prevailing atmosphere of mutual distrust. The period between 1853 and 1889 was marked by constant unrest. Disagreements between civil and military authorities on how best to handle the Indians prevented formulation of a consistent and constructive policy. White settlers and miners appropriated Apache lands with the help of corrupt administrators, and then demanded military

The Gaan dancers of the Apache represent mountain spirits who live in caves near the tops of mountains in Apacheland. They are the guardians and protectors of the Apache people. At one time, they would appear among the Apache during times of great need or difficulty, such as famines and epidemics.

TAD NICHOLS

protection or revenge when the Apache tried to defend their land. Dissident Apache bands frequently left their reservations to pillage Mexican and American settlements, and the peaceable Apaches who stayed on the reservation were often targets for vengeful Anglo raiding parties.

It was not until 1890, after 70 bloody years, that the Apache abandoned their old way of life for more peaceful pursuits.

Today, the Western Apache operate a number of successful tribal enterprises including livestock, lumber mills, recreational areas, resorts, gaming, stores, and service stations. The White Mountain Apache Reservation even supports a public radio station.

Beadwork, cradleboards, and some basketry (primarily burden baskets) are still being produced.

Apache homes tended to be fairly simple affairs that could be quickly built from materials available in the immediate area. This type of brush shelter provided shade from the summer sun and yet allowed cooling breezes to pass through. The Apache were constantly on the move, following the game they hunted as well as the foods that ripened at different times in various areas. Because of this, their dwellings were quite different from the more permanent stone or wood and mud homes of more sedentary tribes.

MARK BAHTI

The scenic and sacred mountainous homeland of the Apache has provided the tribe with timber resources which they carefully manage. It also provides recreational opportunities for Arizona's non-Apache population. Hunting, hiking, fishing, and camping (with permits) are very popular, and the tribe has developed a ski resort as well.

JICARILLA (hee-kah-ree'-yah) — Spanish for "small basket," derived from their production and use of small baskets. Native name is *Tinde*, meaning "the people." Language: Athabascan. Reservation: 823,580 acres. Population: 2,764. Government: Constitution adopted in 1937. Tribal council, chair, and vice-chair elected at large. Ceremonials: Sept. 14-15 - Long Life Ceremony and race (inquire locally for location). ▬▬▬

At the time of Spanish contact the Jicarilla occupied the mountainous region in the vicinity of Taos and Picuris. Their range extended across northern New Mexico and southern Colorado. They had roamed the buffalo plains to the southeast earlier but were driven out, along with the Mescalero, by the Comanche.

From their contact with Pueblo tribes, the Jicarilla learned to supplement their hunting economy with some agriculture. They maintained friendly relations with Picuris and Taos, but did not hesitate to raid the pueblos between peaceful trading visits. Spanish settlements, however, became the primary targets for they provided the Apaches with a source of horses and other livestock. From the Utes, with whom they allied themselves against the Navajo, they acquired a number of Plains Indian traits including buckskin clothing, beadwork, and tipis.

In 1733, the Spaniards established a mission near Taos in an effort to missionize the Jicarilla, who were actually two groups—the *Olleros* (from the Spanish for pottery makers) and the *Llaneros* (Spanish for Plainsmen). It was soon abandoned when the Indians refused to accept a sedentary life under Spanish rule.

Attempts to confine the Jicarilla included a treaty in 1851, which required them to stay at least 50 miles from any settlement. The U.S. government in 1853 attempted to settle several hundred Jicarillas on a reservation on the Rio Puerco. It was unsuccessful, and the Indians continued their forays against the Americans. Between 1853 and 1887, the Jicarilla were moved no less than eight times before the government made up its mind where the tribe should be settled. The boundaries of their new reservation—west of their heartland—were carefully drawn, giving the springs and best land to non-Indians. Schools were set up in 1903, causing an outbreak of tuberculosis to spread to epidemic proportions. An estimated nine in ten Jicarillas suffered from the disease.

Remaining traditional Jicarilla culture is represented by ceremonies like the "Bear Dance" (a long-life ceremony), a girls' puberty rite, and an annual race that re-creates a legendary race between the sun and moon. There has been some revival of older crafts—buckskin, beadwork, and a limited number of coiled baskets are still made.

The Jicarilla derive considerable income from oil and gas leases as well as the sale of timber. This income is invested in education and tribal enterprises that provide jobs for tribal members. A recently opened gaming facility is expected to add to tribal income.

Sheep and cattle raising along with wage work are the primary sources of individual income. Additional tribal income is derived from those who come to camp, hunt, and fish.

Jicarilla Apache baskets with bright aniline dye colors are still woven, though not in the quantity they were made earlier in this century when you could even buy a Jicarilla basketry fishing creel. Photographed at Jicarilla Apache Tribal Co-op

MESCALERO

MESCALERO (mes-kah-ler'-o) — Spanish meaning "mescal people" (for their extensive use of mescal cactus as food). Language: Athabascan. Reservation: 460,678 acres. Population: 3,585. Government: Tribal constitution and bylaws adopted in 1936. Tribe operates under federal charter as a corporation. A business committee of ten, elected biennially by tribal members, functions as a tribal council. Ceremonials: July 1-4 - rodeo and fiesta that includes the appearance of the Gaan (Mountain Spirit) dancers.

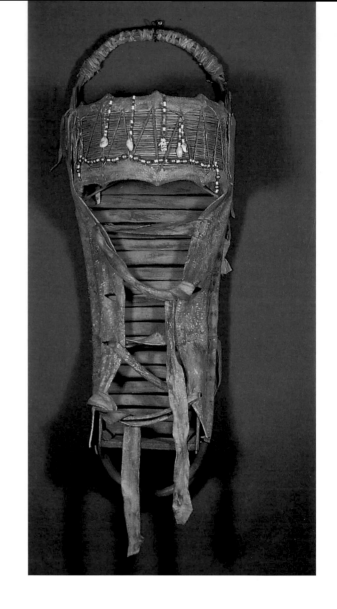

At the time the Spaniards entered the Southwest, the main band of the Mescalero tribe occupied the Sierra Blanca Mountains just north of their present reservation. Other bands inhabited the Big Bend country of Texas and the Guadalupe Mountains of the New Mexico-Texas border.

During the summers they lived in the mountains, moving from one campsite to another in search of game and wild plants. Occasionally they made buffalo hunting trips—using dogs as pack animals before the advent of the horse— onto the plains to the east. During these journeys they frequently fought Comanches who also claimed this territory as their own.

In winter they moved into warmer regions where they made great use of desert plants, par-

Apache buckskin and beadwork is a highly prized craft tradition—especially by the Apache themselves, who are probably the best customers for this type of work. This detail is from a girl's Nah'ih'es dress at the Mescalero–Apache Tribal Museum.

ticularly the mescal cactus, the large tuberous root of which was roasted much like a sweet potato. In between they found time to raid the villages of the Pueblo Indians in the Rio Grande Valley.

Their first contacts with the Spanish explorers were friendly, but the occupation of their land by colonizers soon changed this. By the late 1680s, the Mescalero presented a serious threat to the Spanish settlements in the region.

In 1778-89, the Spanish launched a military campaign to subdue both the Mescalero and the Lipan Apache. Several defeats and the promise of free rations greatly reduced Apache depredations. Relative peace prevailed until 1831 when the Mexican government assumed control of the area. Financial troubles prevented continuance of the ration system, and the Apaches soon left the settlements to resume raiding as a livelihood.

Attempts to confine the Apache were made by the U.S. in the 1850s. Treaties providing "perpetual peace" and rations were made with the Mescalero, but never officially ratified. Raiding, quite naturally, followed and forts were estab-

Apache cradleboards are made not only for collectors, but for use. When hung from a tree or a peg on the wall, infants get to see the world instead of just the ceiling or the treetops, and the snug wrapping makes them feel secure and safe. Photographed at Mescalero–Apache Tribal Museum

Mescalero land is beautiful, but job opportunities are scarce. A casino resort and a racetrack, along with timber and cattle raising, provide income for some. In recent years the tribe has been embroiled in a controversy over whether to open a nuclear waste dump. It has pitted members against one another and involved outsiders as well.

lished in the lower Rio Grande Valley to protect the white settlers.

After a successful military campaign by U.S. troops in 1855, the Mescalero sued for peace and signed a treaty agreeing to settle at Fort Stanton. The experiment was short-lived as peaceful Mescaleros found themselves the victims of raids by revenge-seeking Mexican settlers.

General Carleton finally achieved a military victory over the Mescalero in 1862. In 1864, about 400 were confined to Bosque Redondo near Fort Sumner, New Mexico. The remainder escaped to Mexico or went to live with the Western Apache.

Those who remained at Bosque Redondo suffered greatly. Drought killed their crops and bad water, disease, and Navajo raids decimated their numbers. (In 1864, several thousand Navajos rounded up by Kit Carson were also confined on the 40-square-mile area with the Mescalero.) Once again the Mescalero drifted back to their land and old way of life.

A reservation was established near their home territory in early 1873, but "modified" (read: reduced) later to meet the demands of en-

croaching whites. Programs to "civilize" the Mescalero were designed to destroy the status and influence of the women elders, required the men to cut their hair, and attempted to stop traditional ceremonies and substitute the 4th of July, Thanksgiving, and Christmas for them. Farming was approved as an occupation.

The population of the Mescalero reservation includes members of other Apache tribes—Lipan, Mimbreno, and Chiricahua—the latter arriving in 1913 after their release from prison in Fort Sill, Oklahoma.

Today, most Mescaleros earn their living by wage work on and near the reservation. Tribal income is derived from timber, cattle, a sawmill, a racetrack, a casino, a resort, and recreational activities, which include skiing, hunting, and fishing. A proposal to bring jobs and income by locating a nuclear waste dump on Mescalero land was soundly defeated in 1995, but brought back for a second vote, in which it passed.

Traditional Mescalero crafts are largely limited to cradleboards, beadwork, and a few baskets.

TOHONO O'ODHAM (to'-ho-no ah'-ah-dahm) — native name meaning "desert people." (Formerly Papago, from the Pima name for them, *Papahvi-o-otam,* meaning "bean people.") Language: Piman. Reservations: Tohono O'odham - 2,855,874 acres, San Xavier - 71,095 acres, and Gila Bend - 10,404 acres. Total population: 18,751. Government: Constitution adopted in 1937. Three reservations constitute 11 districts. Adult members of each district elect two persons to tribal council. Tribal officers elected at large. Each district has a five-person council. Celebrations: June 24 - San Juan's Day celebration—dances and chicken pull in some villages. July (no specific dates) - saguaro wine festivals. Oct. 4 - annual pilgrimage to festival in Magdalena, Sonora. Late October - annual rodeo and craft fair.

Today, the Tohono O'odham occupy roughly the same area they inhabited at the time of Spanish contact. The members of this desert tribe are found in widely scattered villages in southern Arizona and northwestern Sonora.

Father Kino began his missionary work among the O'odham in 1687. In addition to a new religion, the Indians acquired European crops from the missions, including winter wheat that eliminated the hunger of the lean winter months. Additionally they gained horses and cattle, quickly becoming proficient cattlemen.

Catholicism, in a modified form which centered about the worship of Saint Francis Xavier as a source of magical power, did not replace native religion but was merely added to it.

ARIZONA STATE MUSEUM

Among the Tohono O'odham of the Sonoran Desert, the June saguaro harvest signaled the beginning of the new year.

Many Tohono O'odham have adobe or contemporary frame or masonry homes, but partially enclosed ramadas are still a feature of most homes. They provide shade during the blistering heat of summer, yet permit cooling breezes to pass through.

Each O'odham village was politically autonomous, led by a headman called "The Keeper of the Smoke." A council of old men discussed village affairs, but took no action until agreement was unanimous. Leaders for hunting and war gained their positions through personal ability and knowledge of rituals (obtained from dreams) necessary for success.

The Round Dance of the Tohono O'odham is often called a Friendship Dance because anyone—tribal member or not, Indian or non-Indian—may join in the circling dance. The singers in the foreground are using traditional instruments—the rattle and basket drum. Catholic missionary efforts are visible in every village, but many traditional values and customs remain, thriving side by side with newer beliefs and customs. Mike Chiago

Traditional Tohono O'odham crafts include pottery and basketry. The pottery originally made was for cooking and storing water. Basketry was used for carrying loads, parching, and storage. Today most pottery and basketry is made for purely decorative purposes. Only a small amount of pottery is made, but the O'odham weave more baskets than all the other tribes combined. Photographed at CRIT Museum

All villages had two locations. From spring until the fall harvest the O'odham lived near the mouth of an arroyo where flash floods supplied moisture for their fields. Cultivating floodplains provides, at best, a precarious livelihood so great use was made of desert plants, particularly the saguaro fruit and mesquite bean. The winter villages were located near mountain springs where the O'odham hunted deer. In time of famine whole families moved north to the Pima villages where they earned their keep by helping the Pimas with their river-irrigated crops.

Tohono O'odham territory came under American control with the Gadsden Purchase in 1853. The Indians lived peacefully under the new government despite occasional skirmishes with white cattlemen who appropriated O'odham grazing land and water holes. For mutual protection against Apache raids they allied themselves with the Anglo settlers.

Because the Tohono O'odham had never fought against the U.S., they had no treaty that would protect them against encroachment by American miners, ranchers, and settlers. They also did not receive the right to vote until 1948. (There's a moral in here somewhere.) In 1874 and 1882, two small reservations were finally set aside for the O'odham at San Xavier and Gila Bend.

In 1917, what is now known as the main reservation—the second-largest reservation in the U.S.—was established. O'odham were forced to leave other areas where they had lived for generations and move to the new reservation. The land they had to leave was among the most productive.

Until 1959, it had the dubious distinction of being the only Indian reservation in which the mineral resources did not belong to the tribe—a testimonial to the power of Arizona's mining industry.

Like the Pima, they also suffered the loss of their water—both surface and underground. The water-hungry growing metropolis of nearby Tucson had wells that began draining the aquifer under Indian land as early as 1881. In 1982, the federal courts awarded them water rights to 76,000 acre-feet, but as of 1995 no water had been delivered.

Many O'odham still weave, due in large part to a bleak employment situation on the reservation. As that improves, weaving will decline—but never disappear, for it is an important aspect of the culture. The apprentice spending long hours with an elder like Frances Manuel learns more than just basketry.

Today, less than one-third of the O'odham live on their reservation year-round. Many leave to find work in nearby towns—others find seasonal jobs in agriculture. Cattle raising and limited farming are the main sources of income for those on the reservation who are not employed by tribal or government agencies, but estimates of the unemployment rate on the reservation range to over 60 percent.

Income from mining leases was once the primary source of revenue for the tribe, but the recent construction of a gaming establishment on the San Xavier reservation near Tucson is proving to be an economic boon for the entire tribe. Plans are being made for further economic development that will provide jobs and housing, and fund social programs and educational opportunities.

The O'odham produce more basketry today than all other tribes combined. Coiled baskets in a variety of shapes and sizes, made of bear grass stitched with yucca and devil's claw, are the most popular. Horsehair miniature baskets are also made, along with some pottery.

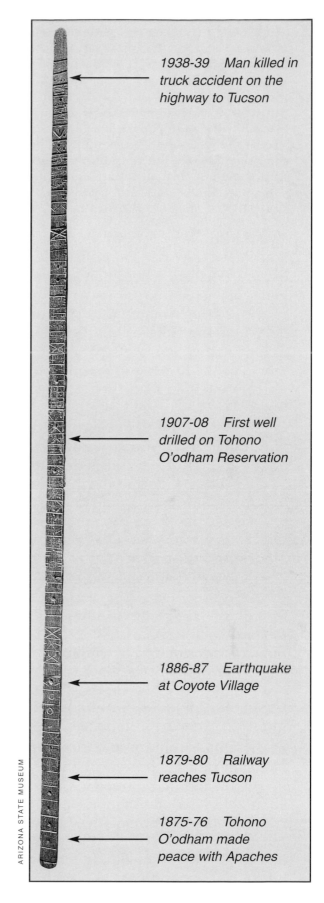

ARIZONA STATE MUSEUM

1938-39   Man killed in truck accident on the highway to Tucson

1907-08   First well drilled on Tohono O'odham Reservation

1886-87   Earthquake at Coyote Village

1879-80   Railway reaches Tucson

1875-76   Tohono O'odham made peace with Apaches

At one time most villages had a calendar stick to mark the significant events that happened over the years. The keeper of such a stick was charged with remembering what each symbol or mark commemorated, and the stick was handed down from one generation to the next. The practice has died out.

YAQUI (yah'-kee) — origin unknown. Native name is *Yoeme*. Language: Piman. Reservation: 995 acres, known as New Pascua, southwest of Tucson. In addition, they occupy four small villages or barrios—two in Tucson, and one each in Marana and Tempe. Population: (Arizona only) 6,227. Government: (New Pascua) tribal council elected by the adult population. Old Pascua village—not a part of the reservation—community buildings owned by the city of Tucson, but controlled by a council consisting of between 30 and 40 village members. Ceremonies: Christmas, Saints' days, and Easter week (which includes deer dancers, *pahkolas, chapayekas,* and *matachines*).

In addition to wearing cocoon rattles and bells, and carrying metal and wood rattles, Yaqui Pahkola dancers are accompanied by a combination flute-player and drummer along with men playing gourd drums and using rasps.

The Yaqui, who occupy five small villages in southern Arizona, are political refugees from Sonora, Mexico, where they originally occupied eight villages.

This tribe of agriculturists numbered about 30,000 at the time of Spanish contact in 1533. Their rancherias were strung out along the full length of the Rio Yaqui. Formidable in battle and fiercely independent, they successfully resisted Spanish efforts to subdue them. Nevertheless, they preferred to live in peace and signed a treaty with the Spaniards in 1610. At the request of the Yaqui, the Jesuits established scattered missions in their settlements and the dispersed population was eventually concentrated into eight towns.

Under the Jesuit program agricultural practices were improved, and livestock and new crops were introduced. The Yaqui were surprisingly receptive to Catholicism and eagerly embraced the new religion. They also accepted the Spanish system of village government, but considered themselves independent of Spanish authority. The Spaniards, reluctant to challenge this powerful tribe, were content to allow the Yaqui to remain autonomous and exempted them from paying tribute. Except for one revolt in 1740, caused by an influx of settlers and a conflict of interest between the Jesuits' program and civil authorities, the Yaqui remained at peace with the Spanish.

After Mexico gained its independence in 1821, it declared the Yaqui to be full citizens of the country. As a practical matter, the change in status meant that the Yaqui lost their sovereignty and had to pay taxes, something they strongly objected to. Combined with new pressures on Yaqui land and water from Mexican settlers and ranchers, it began a period of conflict which continued for over 100 years and ranged from extended guerrilla warfare to full-scale battles. Attempted solutions to the situation included peace offers, wholesale deportation of Yaquis to distant parts of Mexico, and military campaigns to exterminate Yaqui men, women, and children. The last skirmish occurred in 1927. It was during the last 40 years of this period that many Yaquis sought asylum in Arizona.

Because of their political status as refugees, the Yaquis in Arizona were not treated as wards of the U.S. or as a sovereign nation, and so were not entitled to any of the services of the Bureau of Indian Affairs until 1978, when federal legislation gave them recognition as a tribe and a reservation. In 1994 they were finally recognized as a "historic tribe," which then finally gave them the same rights and privileges as other American Indian tribes.

The development of a casino, which draws customers from nearby Tucson, has provided the tribe with employment as well as income to provide better housing and educational opportunities, and to begin planning new economic developments and address the social ills their tribe has endured.

Yaqui religious life, a combination of native and Catholic beliefs and ceremonies, is still very strong. Public performances occur on Saints' days, Easter, and Christmas.

Yaqui beliefs are a mixture of their native religion and Catholicism. Here a Yaqui Pahkola and Deer Dancer genuflect before a very Indian-looking Virgin of Guadalupe. The Maaso or Deer Dancer appears with several Pahkolas during Yaqui Easter observances. A hunt scene is symbolically reenacted with Pahkolas playing the part of hunters. Arturo Montoya

The desert tribes are some of the most impoverished in the Southwest. Recent opportunities to open gambling facilities on the reservations have provided a desperately needed source of income to provide fundamental services like housing, law enforcement, and educational opportunities. The need has deepened with severe cuts in many federal funding sources and services. Many tribes are reinvesting the proceeds in scholarships and economic development.

PIMA (pee'-mah) — from the phrase *pi nyi match*, meaning "I don't know"—the answer given to the Spanish explorers who asked questions in a language they had never heard. The native name is *Akimel O'odham*, meaning "river people." Language: Piman. Reservations: Gila River (shared with the Maricopa) - 371,929 acres, Salt River (shared with the Maricopa) - 66,802 acres, and Ak Chin—meaning "flood plain" (shared with the Tohono O'odham) - 21,840 acres. Population total including Maricopa: 17,091. Government (Ak Chin): Five-member council that elects its own chair and vice-chair. ▬▬▬

Hohokam, a Pima word meaning "those who have gone," is the name given to a remarkable agricultural people who occupied southern and central Arizona for about 1,500 years. Sometime after A.D. 1400 this culture, who had constructed elaborate irrigation systems in the Gila and Salt River valleys, declined and disappeared. Soon afterward they were replaced by Piman-speaking tribes—the Pima and Tohono O'odham, who are possibly descended from the ancient Hohokam.

At the time of Spanish contact the Pima occupied the Gila River Valley. These people were agriculturists who irrigated their farmlands with water diverted from the river. Their population,

estimated at 2,500 in 1775, was concentrated in a number of permanent villages along the river valley. Although they had a strong sense of tribal unity, particularly in time of war, each village was politically independent.

The introduction of livestock and new crops were the only important Spanish contributions to Pima life. Lack of church funds prevented Father Eusebio Kino's mission system from extending to their territory. The impact of a foreign religion was not felt until the late 1800s, when Presbyterian missionaries began working to convert them.

Intensive contact with Anglos began during the Gold Rush when thousands of migrants to California passed through Pima territory. The

The Pima once produced large numbers of very durable willow baskets like this one with a whirlwind pattern called sivalik *in Pima.*

Pima weavers use willow, a more difficult material than the yucca of the Tohono O'odham. As a result, there are far fewer weavers, but the craft is being kept alive.

Indians provided food and supplies for many of the travelers, and relations were consistently friendly.

After the Gadsden Purchase, Anglos began to settle in the rich farmlands of the Gila. Pima's land rights were not recognized until 1859, when a reservation—much smaller than the territory they previously used—was established for them on the Gila. Serious problems began for the Pima when the settlers upstream began to divert water from the Gila River for their own use. Formal protests to Congress proved useless. A tribe that had sold the U.S. Army and settlers an estimated 3 million bushels of surplus wheat in 1870, was so impoverished from water diversion and land theft that by 1895 they had to be issued rations.

A government proposal to relocate them to Oklahoma was rejected. Instead, many of the Pimas moved into the Salt River Valley. To solve the Pimas' water problem, Coolidge Dam was built on the Gila River. The project was a technical success, but once again the legal rights to the water wound up in the hands of non-Indians.

The government's early allotment program resulted in land holdings so fractionalized that, combined with lack of funds to drill wells and government restrictions that permitted only 600 acres to be irrigated, the Pimas were unable to operate successful farms. The Bureau of Indian Affairs, however, approved leasing of Pima land, without such restrictions, to non-Indians.

In 1962, the Ak Chin reservation began to regain control of its farmland. In recent years the tribal farming operation supplied more than 90 percent of the tribal budget, and employed 80 percent of the enrolled populace. The water table, however, drained by nearby Phoenix, began to drop limiting the amount of land they could farm, and prompting Ak Chin to go to Congress to force the government to deliver the water they had promised back in 1912. It finally arrived in 1987.

A casino was opened at Ak Chin in 1994, further enhancing their economic stability and future, and enabling them to begin meeting critical housing needs. An industrial park has opened, and a museum is planned.

The Gila River Reservation was the site of the third-largest internment camp during World War II. The BIA offered the Gila River Reservation as a site for relocating the Japanese without first consulting the tribe, who opposed the arrangement. Intensive negotiations and threats from both the Bureau of Indian Affairs and the War Relocation Authority finally pressured the tribal council into agreement.

Today, the reservation (immediately south of the mushrooming Phoenix metropolitan area) offers a museum, restaurant, and shop complex, which also serves as a job-training site.

The Salt River Reservation (west of Phoenix), home to both Pima and Maricopa, has leased a major discount shopping center—one of the largest in the country—on their land.

MARICOPA (mah-rih-ko'-pah) — derived from the Yuma name for this tribe. The native name is *Piipaash*, meaning "the people." Language: Yuman. Reservations: Gila River (shared with the Pima) - 371,932 acres, and Salt River (shared with the Pima) - 46,619 acres. Population: included in Pima population total. Government: The tribe has no separate tribal government, but participates with the Pima in tribal council organizations on their respective reservations.

The Maricopa tribe originally occupied an area on the lower Colorado River, but was driven out in pre-Spanish times by incessant intertribal warfare and gradually drifted eastward along the Gila River. In 1774, an estimated 1,500 Maricopas inhabited the middle Gila east of the present

Agriculture is still an important source of income for the Pima. This is highly-prized long-staple Pima cotton, domesticated by Indian farmers centuries ago. At one time the Pima produced enormous crop surpluses. In 1870 alone they sold 3 million bushels of wheat to the U.S. Army and settlers. But then their water, and later their best lands were taken from them. By 1895 they had been so impoverished by these thefts that they had to be issued rations to avoid starvation.

town of Gila Bend to the mouth of the Salt River. Under pressure from their traditional enemies, the Mohave and Yuma, they migrated farther east into Pima country.

During the 1800s, they were joined by the remnants of other Yuman tribes who had been driven out of their lower Colorado River territory. These tribes were the Opa (they may have been the same group known as the Maricopa), Halchidhoma, Kahwan, Halyikawamai, Cocomaricopa, and the Kavelchadom (the latter two may have been one and the same). Former identities were submerged into a single group that was referred to collectively as Maricopa, though many on the Salt River Reservation still identify themselves as the Halchidhoma. They allied themselves with the Pima for protection against their common enemies. In 1857, the decisive defeat of a Yuma and Mohave raiding party by the Pima and Maricopa ended their troubles with those two tribes.

In spite of close contact with the Pima, the Maricopa maintained a way of life typical of Colorado River Yumans, among whom dreams were an important source of power. The weaving of cotton blankets on a horizontal loom, and the use of a calendar stick to record events were two of the few traits they did pick up from their neighbors. They produced pottery in quantity, but little basketry.

Little remains of the old culture today. A very small amount of finely polished red pottery, painted with black mesquite sap, is still produced. Native dances, curing rites, traditional tribal organization, and the great emphasis on dreaming for power are all things of the past.

Today, the Maricopa of the Salt River Pima-Maricopa Reservation (established in 1879) and the Gila River Reservation (set aside in 1895) earn their living by subsistence farming, growing cotton and alfalfa, wage work, and leasing land for non-Indian developments, including industrial parks and a motor-sport and recreation facility at Firebird Lake. Most individual land allotments are too small now to be farmed economically, placing the emphasis on tribal farming, overseen by the Maricopa Indian Cooperative Association.

The pottery of many Indian tribes has been influenced by the non-Indian market. This "wedding vase" by Ida Redbird is not a traditional Maricopa shape, but was made to meet the demands of the market.

K. C. DEN DOOVEN

Maricopa pottery, which is very similar to that produced by the neighboring Pima, is usually red on black, but a cream-colored slip is sometimes applied to create a polychrome ware. Mesquite sap is used for the black paint.

Colorado River Tribes

The Yuma, Mohave, Cocopa, and Maricopa are the remaining tribes of a number of closely related groups who occupied the Colorado River and lower Gila River valleys. (Several merged into what are known as the Maricopa by the early 1800s.) They share a common language—Yuman—and a common culture.

These people were primarily agriculturists—crops of corn, beans, and pumpkins were raised on the fertile floodplains of the river. Wild desert plants (especially mesquite beans), small game, and fish supplemented their diet.

The groups maintained a strong sense of tribal identity although they lacked formal political organization. They lived in small, widely separated settlements strung out along the river bottoms. Leaders gained status through their demonstrated abilities, but had no formal authority. Religious ceremonies consisted of individuals singing song cycles that had been "dreamed." Great emphasis was placed on the acquisition of power through dreams. Success in gambling, curing, or war depended solely on this source.

Intertribal warfare was a common occurrence. The acquisition of new farmlands and scalps (a source of supernatural power) led to most fighting. Battles were conducted in a highly formalized manner—long lines of warriors faced each other and, after a warm-up period of shouted insults, engaged in hand-to-hand combat, the favorite weapon being a short, stout club of mesquite wood. Occasionally a champion from each side was selected to settle the dispute.

The dead were disposed of by cremation accompanied by the burning of personal property—a custom that appalled the early white settlers and which the Bureau of Indian Affairs suppressed in favor of a more "civilized" burial.

Contact with the Spanish was very limited and these tribes remained, for the most part, outside the Spanish sphere of influence.

The Treaty of Guadalupe Hidalgo in 1848, and the Gadsden Purchase in 1853, gave the U.S. jurisdiction over these tribes. The tribes objected to the encroachment on their lands by whites, but their mode of warfare was not effective against the tactics and weaponry of the U.S. Army.

Although none of these tribes had treaties with the U.S., reservations were established for them beginning in the 1860s. However, loss of tribal lands to squatters continued as late as 1940, when the Fort Mohave Reservation was opened to settlement by whites.

MOHAVE (mo-hah'-vee), also spelled Mojave.
Mispronunciation of the native name *Aha mahkahve*, meaning "people along the water." Language: Yuman. Reservations: Fort Mohave - 32,697 acres, and Colorado River Indian Reservation (CRIT) (shared with other tribes) - 269,918 acres. Population: 836. Government (Fort Mohave): Tribal affairs are handled by a combination tribal council and business committee elected by tribal members. At CRIT, an intertribal council elected by adult members governs.

The Mohave occupy roughly the same territory today as they did in early times. Their settlements were scattered along the bottomlands on both sides of the Colorado River stretching from Cottonwood Island south to the peaks called "The Needles." According to Mohave tradition they were given the land by their creator, Mutiviyl, who spoke to them through his son Mastamho. At the time of Spanish contact in

Among Yuman tribes rattles were used to accompany a medicine man or shaman's songs. One's right to practice as a shaman came from dreams—the source of all power in Yuman religion.

1776, they numbered about 3,000 although other estimates range as high as 20,000.

Strongly nationalistic and warlike, the Mohave fought with neighboring tribes, and often traveled great distances to make war on other groups. Most of these military expeditions were conducted out of a sense of curiosity about new lands and people rather than to acquire territory or booty. They maintained friendly relations with the Yuma, Chemehuevi, Western Apache, and the Yavapai. They regarded the

Pima, Tohono O'odham, Maricopa, and Cocopa as traditional enemies.

The last major intertribal battle took place in 1857 along the Gila River where Maricopa Indians were attacked by over 100 Mohave and Quechan warriors. After the initial surprise attack, several hundred Pima warriors came to the aid of their Maricopa neighbors and together they nearly annihilated the attackers.

In the 1840s, a wagon trail to the California gold fields ran through Mohave territory. Friction with the immigrants culminated in a full-scale attack on a wagon train in 1858.

The following year Fort Mohave was built to maintain peace. Five Mohave headmen were held as hostages at Fort Yuma as insurance against any outbreak, and then later executed. (The official version of the story is that they were killed while trying to escape.) To impress the Mohave with the futility of further resistance, an important Mohave leader, Irrateba, was sent to Washington, D.C., to observe the great numbers and strength of the Americans. He returned duly impressed and used his influence to convince the Mohaves to remain at peace with the whites and settle on a reservation in the Colorado River Valley in 1858. The conservatives, comprising two-thirds of the tribe, remained behind in Mohave Valley and for decades regarded the Fort Mohave people as "the weak ones."

The Fort Mohave Reservation (which includes parts of California, Nevada, and Arizona) has fewer Mohaves residing there than the Colorado River Indian Reservation (CRIT), which was set aside by the War Department in 1870. During World War II the largest internment camp was established on the CRIT. For this purpose 25,000 acres of their land was appropriated—without tribal consent. After the war, the land was open to settlement by Hopi and Navajo families—many of whom spent their first years in barracks built for the Japanese-Americans imprisoned there. The Mohave and Chemehuevi, fearful of being overwhelmed, voted to stop the immigration in 1952—a move that Congress did not ratify until 12 years later. Increasingly, many descendants of families that moved to CRIT are coming to think of themselves as primarily Mohave. (Current total population is 3001.)

Many Mohaves turned to farming. Others drifted to nearby Anglo communities, particularly Needles, California, to find work. With the development of tribal lands, stock raising and farming have become important economic pursuits. On CRIT the unemployment rate has plummeted due to agricultural jobs, but at Fort Mohave, where much of the farmland is leased to non-Indian agricultural enterprises, the unemployment rate remains staggeringly high. Long-term leasing of some land for non-Indian housing developments, recreation, commercial developments, and a casino promise a better economy for the Fort Mohave people.

Mohave pottery recently died out, but beadwork—including elaborate beaded capes—is still produced. Craftwork, however, has almost no economic importance.

Figurines were extremely popular with tourists and collectors from the late 1800s until well into the 1900s. Now exclusively regarded as collectors' items, they were made for the tourist trade and not for traditional purposes. The markings on the face and body reflect traditional Yuman tattoos. Historic unsigned; photographed at School of American Research

COCOPA (ko'-ko-pah) — name derived from *Kwi-kah-pah*, the Mohave name for this tribe. Language: Yuman. Reservation total (East and West Cocopa): 6,009 acres. Population: 646 (approximately half reside in the Colorado River delta region of Mexico). Government: Tribal council consisting of five members. Constitution adopted in 1964.

The Cocopa, the southernmost of the Yuman tribes, occupied the delta region of the Colorado River. This tribe, divided into three bands, had a total population of 3,000 at the time of Spanish contact in 1540.

They were considered less warlike than the Yuma and Mohave, but often fought with these tribes over territorial disputes. They maintained friendly relations with other neighboring groups with whom they traded for pinyon nuts, acorns, hides, and tobacco. Occasionally captives taken in battle were traded to the Spanish for horses, though children were usually adopted by childless couples.

Dreams were of great importance in predicting the future, and as a source of power. To dream of water ensured success as a warrior; a mockingbird indicated a future as an orator; the appearance of an owl in a dream forebode death. No course of action was taken if a dream predicted anything other than success.

The Cocopa farmed areas of the rich, 50,000-acre Colorado River delta, but also relied heavily on wild desert foods. Fishing and hunting supplemented their diet. When land promoters diverted the Colorado River in 1905 (forming the Salton Sea in California), the delta Cocopa were forced to disperse. Although the river began to flow again after 1907, upstream diversions and polluted runoff from irrigated fields further north destroyed much of their delta land. A crackdown by the U.S. Immigration Service in the 1930s split the tribe into Mexican and American residents.

Today, the Cocopa raise cotton and do some subsistence farming. Land settlements in 1985, which added 4,000 acres to their tiny 500-acre reservation (which was established in 1917), enabled them to farm the land on a commercial basis. Beadwork is the primary craft produced.

Like most Yuman pottery traditions, that of the Mohave has died out or nearly died out several times in the last 40 years. During most of that time, when pottery was being produced, it was usually the work of a single artist. Currently there are no active potters among the Mohave. Elmer Gates; photographed at CRIT Museum

YUMA (yoo'-mah) — derived from *Yum*, the Pima name for this tribe. Native name is *Quechan*, a reference to the trail they followed in leaving *Wi Kahme*, Spirit Mountain, from which all Yuman tribes are believed to have emerged. Language: Yuman. Reservation: Fort Yuma - 43,561 acres. Most of this reservation lies in California— only about 480 acres are in Arizona. Population: 2,234, of whom fewer than 100 live in Arizona. Government: Adult members elect a president, vice-president, and five-member council.

The Yuma, or Quechan as they prefer to be known, occupied the Colorado River between the territories held by the Cocopa and Mohave.

Early Spanish contact was limited to a brief visit by Hernando de Alarcon, who sailed up the Colorado River to Yuma country in 1540. Kino paused in the Quechan villages during his trip to California in 1698 only long enough to distribute "canes of authority" to a few leaders.

In 1779, the Franciscans sent Padre Garces with a military escort to establish missions in Quechan territory. The Indians, who had proved to be friendly when treated as equals, resisted this attempt to subjugate them. They were unwilling to give up either land or independence in return for the dubious benefits of a new religion. In 1781, Quechans destroyed the mission (located near the present town of Yuma) and killed the priests and soldiers. Except for the introduction of new crops, Spanish contact had no influence on Quechan culture.

The discovery of gold in California resulted in an invasion of Quechan lands by thousands of "forty-niners" on their way to the goldfields. Despite raids on their farm plots by the migrants, and the pilfering from wagon trains by the Indians, the situation remained relatively peaceful.

Some enterprising Quechans even constructed rafts and provided ferry service to transport the white men across the Colorado River.

Any attempt to settle on Quechan lands, however, met with opposition. The earliest difficulties arose when Anglos tried to establish a ferry service in competition with the Quechans. By 1850, the Americans were demanding "protection" from the Indians, and a military outpost was established at Camp Yuma. The small detachment kept hostilities to a minimum, but failed to prevent the whites from taking Quechan land.

Hostilities soon broke out, and the army proceeded to subdue the Quechan. This was done not by military engagements, but through the destruction of Yuma fields and settlements, most of which were then regarded as "abandoned" and taken over by white settlers.

A reservation was established in 1883 but thrown open to settlement by non-Indians the following year, and a new reservation was set aside, with much of the land arid and unsuited for agriculture. Less than ten years later this reservation was severely cut in size. Finally, in 1978, the tribe regained control of nearly 25,000 acres of their land, though water rights to the land were not included and some of the choicest parcels remained in non-Indian hands. In 1914, tribal members living south of the border fled civil unrest to join their northern kin in what had become the U.S., avoiding the tribal separation many other border tribes endure.

A few women still produce beaded items ranging from belts and pendants to elaborate capes, but virtually no other traditional crafts survive.

CHEMEHUEVI (chem-eh-hway'-vee) — the Yuman name for the Paiutes of southeastern California. Native name is *Nuhwuh*, meaning "the people." Language: Shoshonean. Reservation: Colorado River (shared with several other tribes) - 265,850 acres, of which 225,995 are in Arizona and 39,855 in California. Population: 95. Government: Constitution adopted in 1937. Tribal officers selected by a nine-member council. Council members elected biennially for four-year terms.

The use of present-day political boundaries to identify and locate Indian tribes in prehistoric times does more to confuse than enlighten. State lines are generally accepted as logical dividing lines for closely related tribes, and little regard is shown for natural geographic boundaries that cross the neat but imaginary lines drawn on maps.

Thus it is that the Chemehuevi are usually listed as a "California desert tribe," when in reality they are linguistically and culturally part of the Great Basin culture which occupied the major portion of what is now Nevada and Utah.

A small tribe of about 800, they led a semi-nomadic life in the eastern half of the Mojave Desert. Extensive use of wild plants supplemented by small game allowed the Chemehuevi to eke out an existence in this inhospitable region. Small bands, sometimes no more than an extended family unit, ranged over wide areas to gather sufficient quantities of seeds, roots, and berries. It was much more practical to move a camp to the food supply than maintain permanent settlements. The necessity to roam did not permit the development of strong tribal unity, complex social organization, or elaborate rituals and ceremonies.

In the late 1700s, the Chemehuevi moved into Mohave territory on the west side of the Colorado River. This contact resulted in the acquisition of a number of Yuman traits including mourning ceremonies, dreaming for power, and much of Mohave mythology.

In 1867, hostilities disrupted their friendly relations with the Mohave, and the Chemehuevi withdrew to the desert country to the west. Later, however, they drifted back to occupy the Chemehuevi Valley.

A reservation was set aside for this tribe on the California side of the Colorado River, but the construction of Parker Dam in 1938 caused much of the arable land to be flooded. Most of the Chemehuevi then moved to the Colorado River Indian Reservation.

A resort in California, reached by ferry from Lake Havasu City, Arizona, is now an important source of tribal income and employment, surpassing that from the growing of alfalfa and cotton.

Once noted for fine coiled baskets of willow and devil's claw, the craft has nearly disappeared. Native ceremonies have also disappeared.

Chemehuevi basketry has long been admired for its fine coils and tight stitching. The number of weavers active in this very demanding, time-intensive craft has steadily and predictably dwindled. At the moment there is only one master weaver, and she has a single apprentice.

MARK BAHTI

Hualapai twined basketry was on the verge of disappearing in the late 1960s when there were only a few active weavers—mostly elderly—and no one in the younger generation seemed interested in learning the craft. A rebirth of interest beginning about 1970 resulted in a number of new weavers.

HUALAPAI (wah'-lah-pai), also spelled Walapai
— derived from the native name *Hawwahlah pa'a*, meaning "pine mountain people." Language: Yuman. Reservations: Peach Springs and Big Sandy - 992,163 acres. Population: 1,498. Government: Constitution adopted in 1938. Tribal council made up of eight elected members and one hereditary chief chosen by subchiefs of each band. Tribal officers are selected by the council. ▬▬▬

Originally 13 bands of the Pai, or *Pa'a* ("the people"), occupied the area north of the Mohave on the upper Colorado River in what is now northwestern Arizona. Long before the Spanish entered the Southwest they had moved eastward into the plateau region. From this original group there emerged three separate tribes—Hualapai, Yavapai, and Havasupai. Linguistically they are related to the Colorado River Yumans, and trace their migration back to the Yuman emergence from Spirit Mountain, but culturally they are closer to the Southern Paiute.

The territory of the Hualapai (who were comprised of two Pai bands) included the area between Bill Williams River and the Grand Canyon, and west almost to the Colorado River.

The Hualapai were a small tribe whose total population did not exceed 1,000. Their tiny settlements, usually consisting of two or three families, were scattered over the arid plateau wherever a permanent water supply was located. The Hualapai practiced a limited amount of agriculture, but were primarily dependent upon game and wild plants for food.

Although they were not particularly warlike, they occasionally fought with the Paiute and Yavapai. Friendly trade relations were maintained with the Mohave and the Hopi, with whom they exchanged buckskins for foodstuffs, and even with the Navajo, from whom they obtained blankets.

Contact with the Spanish was limited to one brief visit by Father Garces in 1776, so trouble with foreigners had to wait until the arrival of the Americans in 1852.

At first, relations with the Americans were peaceful, but in 1865 the Pai War (which included the Havasupai and the Yavapai) began when miners and cattlemen began to appropriate Hualapai springs and waterholes. The government was unwilling to defend Hualapai rights so, under the guise of avoiding bloodshed, the Indians were force-marched in 1874 to the Colorado River and placed on the Mohave Reservation near Parker, Arizona, thereby allowing whites to take over their land. Unaccustomed to the intense heat of the region they faced starvation, spoiled rations, and epidemics before the survivors moved back to their old homeland—which no longer belonged to them. Destitute, they were forced to accept government rations to survive. In 1883, a reservation was set aside for them in their native country, but it was made up of areas that the whites had found unsuitable.

Because the Hualapai were no longer at war and therefore not dangerous, they were regarded by the Americans merely as an intolerable nuisance. One newspaper, the *Mojave County Miner*, suggested editorially in 1887 that rations for the Indians be mixed with "a plentiful supply of arsenic" to solve the "problem." The army, which hired many Hualapais as scouts in their battles with the Apache, became concerned for the welfare of its valued scouts and recommended that the Hualapai be given a reservation. In 1884, nearly a million acres of rough country was set aside for them. Even so, much of their land was leased to non-Indian ranchers—with none of the revenue going to the Hualapai.

Under the circumstances it is little wonder that the Hualapai eagerly took part in the Ghost Dance—a messianic movement started by Wovoka, a Paiute medicine man. For two years the prescribed dances were performed in the belief that they would result in the return of Indian dead and the disappearance of the troublesome whites. Unfortunately (depending upon your point of view), they failed.

Stock raising is the main livelihood for the Hualapai today. Except for limited acreage on the Big Sandy Reservation, most of the tribal land is unsuited for farming. Tribal income is derived mainly from timber sales, with some also gained from the limited sale of bighorn sheep hunting permits ($20,000 each), and fees for river running, camping, and hiking. All travel off the state highway on Hualapai land requires a permit. Because of limited natural resources most Hualapais must leave the reservation to earn a living. The unemployment rate is estimated as high as 70 percent. The tribe hopes to build a major resort.

A casino was established to generate income to reinvest in an economic development program, but lack of visitation to their isolated reservation forced them to close it after less than a year in operation.

In 1976, in an effort to maintain Hualapai language and culture, the tribe instituted a bilingual, bicultural program for the tribe's children. Enormously successful, it has become a national model for other tribes.

Basketry, the only remaining craft, continues to be produced in limited quantity. All Hualapai basketry employs a diagonal twining technique; bands of simple geometric patterns in aniline dye colors are the only decoration.

YAVAPAI (yah'-vah-pai) — from *Enyava-pai*, meaning "people of the sun." Language: Yuman. Reservations: Yavapai - 1,559 acres, Camp Verde (shared with the Tonto Apache) - 653 acres, and Fort McDowell (shared with Apache) - 24,680 acres. Population total: 703. Government: (Yavapai) Community council with elected chair. (Camp Verde) Constitution adopted in 1938. Tribal members elect eight-person community council which in turn elects chair and vice-chair. (Fort McDowell) Constitution adopted in 1936. Tribal members elect a five-member community council.

The Yavapai claimed as their territory the area from the Verde Valley to the Colorado River between the Gila and Bill Williams rivers. The tribe, which probably numbered no more than 1,500, was divided into four subtribes, each comprised of a number of bands.

According to their tradition, the Yavapai once formed a single tribe with the Hualapai, but intratribal conflict brought about a split. After that time the Hualapai were regarded as enemies along with the Havasupai, Maricopa, and Pima. They maintained friendly relations with the Western Apache, particularly the Tonto band with whom they frequently intermarried. As a result, the Yavapai have often (and confusingly) been referred to as the Yavapai-Apache, as well as Mojave-Yavapai and Yuma-Apache. The fine coiled baskets they once produced and are famous for, were a craft they learned from the Apache.

Unlike their Yuman-speaking relatives on the Colorado River, the Yavapai did not practice agriculture but instead led a semi-nomadic existence, subsisting entirely by hunting and gathering wild foods. Dwellings were caves as well as brush shelters similar to Apache wickiups.

Contact with the Spanish was very slight, and the Yavapai managed to remain beyond the reach of both the Church and the Crown.

In the 1860s, their territory was invaded by Anglo prospectors and miners. Bloody feuds and massacres resulted, and continued until both the Yavapai and the Apache were defeated by General Crook in 1872. Settling on their new reservation, they managed to hand dig a five-mile canal to irrigate their 50 arable acres.

Their first harvest was such a success that the army contractors who had been supplying substandard (and often shortchanged) rations were afraid the Yavapai might become self-sufficient. Their complaints were heard, and the following year the 1,000 Yavapais gathered at Camp Verde were force-marched 150 miles to the San Carlos

Reservation. Many died along the way or were murdered by the soldiers—a few managed to escape. They remained there for 25 years before being allowed to return to their home country.

Some settled at Fort McDowell (established as a reservation in 1903) when they discovered that their traditional lands had been taken over by white settlers. Others returned to Camp Verde where a small reservation was established for them in 1914. In 1935, a third reservation, 75 acres in size, was set aside for them near Prescott. The town had now grown to the edges of the reservation, providing the Yavapai with badly needed income from the development and leasing of their lands. The westernmost subtribe were never given back any of their land.

The most famous member of the tribe was Wassaja, born in 1865, taken captive by the Pima as a young boy, and then bought by an Anglo who renamed him Carlos Montezuma. He earned a medical degree, published a newspaper, and was a tireless and eloquent advocate of the Indian. Montezuma argued for the abolishment of what was then known as the Indian Bureau, saying it worked against Indian rights, self determination, and self-sufficiency.

Camp Verde (which includes land at the Middle Verde and in Clarkdale) relies upon agriculture for its income, while the Yavapai near Prescott have an industrial park, shopping center, resort hotel, and gaming operation.

The Fort McDowell Reservation has limited resources, with only a tiny amount of land suitable for farming and grazing. While their relatives in Camp Verde were having to fight for enough water to irrigate their land, the Fort McDowell people had to fight being inundated by it. Orme Dam threatened for decades to flood the last of their best land before the project was shelved.

The Yavapai and Apache people of Fort McDowell opened the first Indian gaming operation in Arizona. It is a good example of the effect gaming has had on tribes in the Southwest and how they have handled the income derived from it. Unemployment rates have dropped from a highly conservative 28 percent in 1989 to virtually zero by 1994. Differing from several other tribes, 34 percent of the casino's revenue is distributed directly to adult tribal members (or into savings for those under age 18, who must graduate from high school or obtain a GED before they have access to their account—otherwise they must wait until age 21). Tribal operations, including health, housing, and economic development projects split 60 percent, and 6 percent goes to support charitable causes off-reservation.

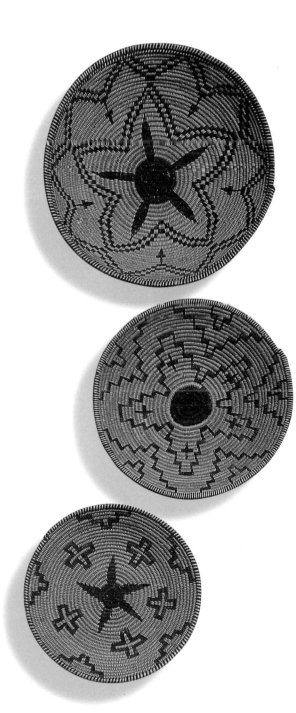

Yavapai Apache coiled basketry is highly sought after by collectors and prized for its design work which ranges from highly intricate to very simple yet elegant. Working with willow coiled basketry is a difficult and demanding craft that requires years to master. Unfortunately, it has died out among the Yavapai.

HAVASUPAI

HAVASUPAI (hah-vah-suu'-pai) — from the native name *Hawasuwaipaa*, which means "people of the blue-green water." (Also referred to as *Supai* and *Coconino*—the Hopi name for these people.) Language: Yuman. Reservation: 188,077 acres. Population: 591. Government: Constitution adopted in 1939. Tribal council made up of four elected council members and three hereditary chiefs selected by subchiefs. Tribal officers selected by council. Ceremonies: Harvest Dance in late summer.

The Havasupai, a branch of the Hualapai, separated from the main tribe during the 12th century to seek refuge from potential enemies, and moved to the very bottom of the Grand Canyon. Today, they are still the most isolated tribe in the U.S. Other than by helicopter, their reservation can be reached only on foot or by horseback over two long trails that lead down from the rim.

In early days the Havasupai occupied the canyon bottom only during the spring and summer months to farm their tiny gardens. In the fall, after the harvest, they moved to their winter dwellings on the plateau where they hunted deer, antelope, and mountain sheep. (The Navajo stopped their eastward expansion and drove them out of the Colorado River Basin area

HOWARD BOOTH

Flooding in 1993 changed the appearance of many scenic areas in Havasu Canyon and caused considerable destruction on the reservation, requiring long-term restoration.

after a final battle in 1638.) During the winter months the land along the river bottom becomes bitterly cold and damp as the steep canyon walls shut out the sunshine.

Life among the Havasupai was simple. Rigid social and political organization was hardly necessary for a group with a population of less than 300. Religious activities were in the hands of medicine men who controlled the weather, treated illnesses, and ensured success in hunting and farming. A fall harvest dance was more a social activity than a religious ceremony. Cremation of the dead and the destruction of the deceased's personal property (one of several customs this tribe has in common with other Yuman tribes)

JEFF GNASS

The travertine pools of Havasu Canyon have long been a significant attraction for visitors from around the world. The blue-green color of the waters give the tribe their name— Hawasuwaipaa, *People of the Blue-Green Water.*

was practiced until 1895, when the Bureau of Indian Affairs forbade this "uncivilized" practice.

Despite their isolation the Havasupai had considerable contact with the Hopi, trading buckskins, salt, mountain sheep horns, and red mineral paint for agricultural products, textiles, and pottery. Father Garces (in 1776) was the only Spaniard to visit this tribe. Plans to missionize the tribe failed to materialize. Contact with Americans, which began in the 1850s, was equally unimportant. No one, it seemed, coveted the isolated homeland of the Havasupai.

In 1882, a reservation of 512 acres was established for the tribe in Havasu Canyon. The Havasupai refrained from requesting a larger tract (which they had traditionally occupied and used) in the belief that holding title to a greater area would only invite trouble with the Americans—a tiny reservation would be no temptation to even the most land-hungry white man.

Much of their traditional land, including the area known as Indian Gardens, was taken away from them when Grand Canyon National Park was established. Though many continued to stay on, working for the National Park Service, their traditional homes were destroyed and they were forced to rent cabins. In 1975, they were given back 185,000 acres of their homeland, plus exclusive rights to use 95,300 acres in Grand Canyon National Park. There are, however, significant restrictions on how they may utilize their 185,000 acres, and even a limit on how much money they can make from its use! Ironically, the U.S. government has allowed a uranium mine to be developed upstream from the Havasupai by non-Indians on federal land—with no similar restrictions.

Although often referred to as a "Shangri-la" by the casual visitor, the reservation is considerably less idyllic to those who live there. Agriculture, once the main occupation of the tribe, today only supplements the income derived from outside wage work and some leasing of grazing land. A few Havasupai earn a livelihood by providing transportation (horses and mules) and accommodations to visitors to their canyon. Tourism is the major source of income for the tribe.

Baskets, in both twined and twilled techniques, are still produced by the Havasupai, but in very limited quantities.

Havasu Canyon, where the Havasupai Reservation is located, is a fraction of the land the Indians once used. In 1975 the Havasupai were officially given back much of their homeland and granted permission to use several thousand acres in the Grand Canyon—but in both cases, a limit was placed upon how much money they could make from its use!

KAIBAB PAIUTE (pi'-yoot or pah'-yoot) —
which may come from the words *Pai-ute*, "true Ute," or *Pah-ute*, "water Ute." Also known as the *Nuwuvi*. Native name for this band (one of over 30) is *Kaivahn-eetseng*, "mountain lying down people." Language: Shoshonean. Reservation: 120,827 acres. Population: 205. Government: Constitution adopted 1951. Members elect a six-person tribal council. Council selects tribal officers who operate in conjunction with a committee of elders. Other bands of Paiute occupy reservations in Utah and Nevada. ▬▬▬▬

The Kaibab band, a branch of the Southern Paiute, originally ranged over portions of northwestern Arizona, southern Utah, and southeastern Nevada beginning about A.D. 1150. Their original territory covered approximately 5,000 square miles that varied from lush to barren.

The economy of the Paiute was based on food gathering. They led a semi-nomadic existence in order to make maximum use of whatever wild foods were available. Their extensive use of edible roots earned them the name of "Diggers" from contemptuous Anglos, but even the most ethnocentric settler had to admit that the Paiutes could exist in lands where a white man would quickly starve to death. Nothing was overlooked—pine nuts, wild grass seeds, even grasshoppers and caterpillars were eaten. Over 100 species of plants were utilized as food and still others for medicinal purposes. Big game was scarce so the Indians hunted rabbits, birds, gophers, prairie dogs, and mice.

Life for the Paiute was a constant search for food, and it left little time to develop elaborate crafts or social or religious organizations. The land would not support large concentrations of people, so most groups consisted of two or three families. Leaders had no formal authority over their followers, relying on the consensus of the group. Medicine men conducted brief hunting and curing rituals.

The Kaibab Paiute had some contact with Utes and learned from them the use of buckskin clothing, the horse, and the tipi, which replaced their earlier earth-covered lodges.

Encroachment by Mormon settlers began in the early 1860s. If land claimed and used by the semi-nomadic Paiute happened to be unoccupied at the time a settler arrived, it was claimed and fenced, and the Paiute prevented from ever using it again. In this manner they lost most of their land. Poor land management practices by the settlers started erosion that caused the once-lush Kaibab region with abundant surface water to dry up and rely heavily on ever-deeper wells.

ARIZONA HISTORICAL SOCIETY

Before Captain John Wesley Powell led his famous exploration of the Grand Canyon in 1869, he consulted with the Kaibab Paiute who were quite familiar with the canyon.

Permanent water sources on the Kaibab Plateau are few and far between. Pitch-covered basketry bottles were made to collect and store water.

By the time a reservation was finally established for them in 1909, European-introduced illnesses combined with the loss of their best lands had decimated the tribe, reducing their numbers by 90 percent.

The land set aside for their reservation is marginally suitable for some cattle raising and limited agriculture. A casino was established to generate income for an economic development program, but their remote isolated location resulted in its closure.

Buckskin and basketry were the two main crafts of the Kaibab band. Burden baskets, trays for winnowing, bowls for parching wild seeds, and hats were made using a twining technique. Coiled baskets in bowl and bottle shapes are made of sumac.

The "wedding basket" (actually used in a variety of ceremonies) is made by the San Juan Paiute, a group of Southern Utes who moved into the San Juan area which is now a part of the Navajo reservation. The San Juan Utes are generally counted as Navajos by the government, and have been struggling for recognition (recently awarded) and autonomy. They now have a tribal headquarters in Tuba City, Arizona, but the land on which they live is still part of the Navajo reservation.

The extensive Kaibab Plateau was home to the Kaibab band of the Southern Paiute. Typical of the experience of most tribes, the best land was quickly taken by settlers. The land they now have supports a limited cattle operation and garden plots.

The lands of the Southwestern Indian tribes have shaped them in many ways. In turn, the hand of the Indian has left its mark on the Southwest. *Mary Lovato*

SUGGESTED READING

CUSHING, FRANK H. *The Nation of Willows.* Flagstaff, Arizona: Northland Press, 1965.

DOZIER, EDWARD. *The Pueblo Indian of North America.* New York, New York: Holt, Rinehart and Winston, 1968.

EVERS, LARRY, ed. *Between Sacred Mountains.* Tucson: Sun Tracks and the University of Arizona Press, 1982.

LOCKE, RAYMOND F. *The Book of the Navajo.* Los Angeles, California: Mankind Publishing, 1976.

LOCKWOOD, FRANK. *The Apache Indians.* Lincoln: University of Nebraska Press, 1938.

NEQUATEWA, EDMUND. *Truth of a Hopi: Stories Relating to the Origin, Myths, and Clan Histories of the Hopi.* Flagstaff, Arizona: Northland Press, 1967.

PARSONS, ELSIE C. *Pueblo Indian Religion.* (2 vols.) Lincoln: University of Nebraska Press, 1996.

REID, JEFFERSON and STEPHANIE WHITTLESEY. *The Archaeology of Ancient Arizona.* Tucson: University of Arizona Press, 1997.

SHERIDAN, THOMAS E. and NANCY PAREZO, eds. *Paths of Life—American Indians of the Southwest and Northern Mexico.* Tucson: University of Arizona Press, 1996.

SPICER, EDWARD H. *The Yaquis: A Cultural History.* Tucson: University of Arizona Press, 1980.

SPICER, EDWARD H. *Cycles of Conquest.* Tucson: University of Arizona Press, 1962.

STOFFLE, RICHARD and MICHAEL EVANS. *Kaibab Paiute History.* Fredonia, Arizona: Kaibab Paiute Tribe, 1978.

TRIMBLE, STEVE. *The People—Indians of the American Southwest.* Santa Fe, New Mexico: SAR Press, 1993.

WEBB, GEORGE. *A Pima Remembers.* Tucson: University of Arizona Press, 1959.

ZUNI PEOPLE. *The Zunis: Self Portrayals.* Albuquerque: University of New Mexico Press, 1972.

The Publisher gratefully acknowledges the use of original paintings from the following galleries and museums: Amerind Foundation, Inc.; James T. Bialac Collection; Elvis Torres Gallery; Simons Collection; and Oliver Enjady's private collection. Items photographed in this Southwestern Indian Trilogy came from numerous shops, museums, private collections, and individual Indian artisans. The work represents the broad range of items available for sale at reputable Indian arts and crafts shops nationwide.

Inside back cover: Ancient traditions and beliefs still provide much of the strength and values which enable Indian people to enter the future. Photo by Mark Bahti of a restored prehistoric kiva.

Back cover: Nah-ahtseh elit, the Rainbow, protects sandpaintings used in Navajo healing ceremonies. Photo by K. C. DenDooven.

Created, Designed, and Published in the U.S.A.
Printed by Tien Wah Press (Pte.) Ltd, Singapore
Pre-Press by United Graphic Pte. Ltd